NEW DIRECTIONS FOR COMMUNITY COLLEGES

Arthur M. Cohen
EDITOR-IN-CHIEF

Florence B. Brawer
ASSOCIATE EDITOR

Curriculum Models for General Education

George Higginbottom
Broome Community College

Richard M. Romano
Broome Community College

EDITORS

Number 92, Winter 1995

JOSSEY-BASS PUBLISHERS
San Francisco

ERIC®

Clearinghouse for Community Colleges

CURRICULUM MODELS FOR GENERAL EDUCATION
George Higginbottom, Richard M. Romano (eds.)
New Directions for Community Colleges, no. 92
Volume XXIII, number 4
Arthur M. Cohen, Editor-in-Chief
Florence B. Brawer, Associate Editor

Microfilm copies of issues and articles are available in 16mm and 35mm, as well as microfiche in 105mm, through University Microfilms Inc., 300 North Zeeb Road, Ann Arbor, Michigan 48106-1346.

LC 85-644753   ISSN 0194-3081   ISBN 0-7879-9938-5

NEW DIRECTIONS FOR COMMUNITY COLLEGES is part of The Jossey-Bass Higher and Adult Education Series and is published quarterly by Jossey-Bass Inc., Publishers, 350 Sansome Street, San Francisco, California 94104-1342 in association with the ERIC Clearinghouse for Community Colleges. Second-class postage paid at San Francisco, California, and at additional mailing offices. POSTMASTER: Send address changes to New Directions for Community Colleges, Jossey-Bass Inc., Publishers, 350 Sansome Street, San Francisco, California 94104-1342.

SUBSCRIPTIONS for 1995 cost $49.00 for individuals and $72.00 for institutions, agencies, and libraries.

THE MATERIAL in this publication is based on work sponsored wholly or in part by the Office of Educational Research and Improvement, U.S. Department of Education, under contract number RI-93-00-2003. Its contents do not necessarily reflect the views of the Department, or any other agency of the U.S. Government.

EDITORIAL CORRESPONDENCE should be sent to the Editor-in-Chief, Arthur M. Cohen, at the ERIC Clearinghouse for Community Colleges, University of California, 3051 Moore Hall, 405 Hilgard Avenue, Los Angeles, California 90024-1521.

Cover photograph © Rene Sheret, After Image, Los Angeles, California, 1990.

Manufactured in the United States of America on Lyons Falls Pathfinder Tradebook. This paper is acid-free and 100 percent totally chlorine-free.

CONTENTS

EDITORS' NOTES

Much of the literature on the topic of general education at the community college is concerned with its curricular evolution and definition and with justifications for its inclusion in degree programs. Although the contributors to this volume of New Directions comment incisively upon general education's aims and rationale, their focus is on the process of curriculum reform at the campus and system level. Curriculum leaders at seven community colleges and one community college system chronicle their experiences with general education reform. Through these narratives, we have sought to provide a practical guide and reference for those seeking to reexamine or restructure their own general education programs. We hope that the eight representative models presented in this volume will provide others with a clearer picture of how general education is actually undertaken at the community college level.

The programs are presented in alphabetical order. Each contributor was asked to use a standard format. Included are brief descriptions of each college, including its internal culture and environmental constraints; the general education program, its aims and evolution; implementation and assessment problems; and a reflective appraisal on lessons learned. The final chapter, Concluding Remarks, discusses the intellectual foundations of the general education movement and appraises the eight models presented in this volume in light of contemporary general education trends.

Distinguishing Features

The one prerequisite for inclusion in this volume was that a college's general education program had to be comprehensive. Programs were considered comprehensive if general education goals were incorporated into all an institution's degree programs. Beyond this, as you read these narratives, you will find both similarities and differences among them. We have found the following features of the curriculum change process at these institutions especially interesting:

Black Hawk Community College (Illinois): the DACUM process as a means of defining and clarifying general education goals and ensuring faculty ownership of the program
Broome Community College (New York): the role of co-curricular programming in reinforcing and extending curricular learning as well as the prominence of civic education
Bunker Hill Community College (Massachusetts): their close attention to a fully participative process and planning for assessment

Jefferson Community College (Kentucky): how systemwide competencies are translated into particular course and curriculum requirements for community college students

Miami-Dade Community College (Florida): the Wolfson campus's thematically integrative models and their incorporation into the general education core

Minnesota Community Colleges: both the scale of the commitment to the participative process and the painstaking, systemwide specification of goals and competencies

Piedmont Community College (Virginia): their success in garnering grant money in support of general education reform; in particular, a National Endowment for the Humanities-funded interdisciplinary humanities course

Shoreline Community College (Washington): the twenty learning outcomes and, especially, the curriculum and instructional design that incorporates learning communities and integrated studies

Method of Selection

We selected eight comprehensive general education programs for inclusion in this volume using the following approach. First, we sent letters to every public and private two-year college in the United States, inviting each to submit a description of their program for consideration. We received more than five hundred responses. Second, letters were sent to all state community college offices, inviting institutional nominations. We also asked researchers in the field for their nominations. Last, we searched the literature on community college general education for likely candidates.

From these responses we compiled a list of eighty-seven colleges that claimed to have comprehensive general education programs. Subsequently, we reviewed the materials provided and selected for inclusion the colleges contained in this volume. In the selection of institutions we have attempted to provide some geographical diversity, as well as variety in both programs and community college governance arrangements. No doubt we have omitted many worthy and interesting programs in limiting those profiled to eight, but we are very pleased to present to our colleagues engaged in general education curriculum reform this group of exemplary models.

George Higginbottom
Richard M. Romano
Editors

GEORGE HIGGINBOTTOM is dean of the Division of Liberal Arts and Related Careers at Broome Community College in Binghamton, New York. He is a founding member and past president of the Community College General Education Association.

RICHARD M. ROMANO is professor of economics and long-time General Education Steering Committee member at Broome Community College. He is also the director of the Institute for Community College Research.

Black Hawk College demonstrates a comprehensive approach to general education. The college used a DACUM process to clearly identify the desired outcomes of general education for all degree graduates.

General Education in the Heartland: Black Hawk College

Dorothy R. Martin, Sheila Lillis

Black Hawk College is located in the heartland of the upper Mississippi Valley in northwestern Illinois. The district covers 2,164 square miles and serves approximately 7,500 students for an FTE of 4,100 per semester. Black Hawk College operates two campuses—a rural campus in Kewanee and an urban campus in Moline. The college opened in 1946 as an extension of the University of Illinois. In 1948, it became Moline Community College, operated by Moline K–12 School District No. 40. Then, in 1962, it became a two-year comprehensive community college operating under the authority of its own board of trustees. From its beginnings, the college has emphasized its University Parallel Program. In the early 1960s, the college began to expand its course offerings to include career programs. Today the college offers more than sixty different career programs in addition to its transfer and outreach adult education programs.

Rationale/Description of General Education Program

The college's general education philosophy reflects its beginnings as an extension of a four-year institution. Embedded in that philosophy has always been the commitment to providing transfer students with a broad knowledge base. Today, Black Hawk, like most community colleges, integrates the traditional liberal arts knowledge base with skills that facilitate communicative and quantitative competence, critical thinking, problem-solving, flexibility, and lifelong learning.

The current general education program at Black Hawk College consists of six categories of discipline distribution requirements: communications, humanities, social sciences, natural sciences, quantitative studies, and non-Western studies. The descriptions of each area and examples of courses in that area are as follows:

Communications. Courses in this area enhance the fundamental skills of effective writing, reading, listening, and speaking essential to all fields of work. Courses include composition and speech.

Humanities. Courses in this area broaden a student's cultural experience and knowledge and develop an appreciation of the fine arts. Courses include modern fiction, American literature, foreign languages, art and music appreciation, philosophy, logic, and history of Western civilization.

Social sciences. Courses in this area expand students' awareness of relationships among populations and societies and provide an understanding of our cultural heritage and the interaction of social systems. Courses include U.S. history, government, introductory psychology and sociology, anthropology, and micro- and macroeconomics.

Natural sciences. Courses in this area contribute to the students' understanding of the scientific method of inquiry and introduce them to the growing body of knowledge about the natural world. Courses include astronomy, general biology, inorganic chemistry, geology, and physics.

Quantitative studies. Courses in this area allow students to develop and sharpen their skills in analysis, quantification, and synthesis. Courses include computer science, college algebra, and trigonometry, calculus, and statistics.

Non-Western studies. Courses in this area provide students with background knowledge of social, political, and cultural development in Third World or non-Western cultures. Courses include international business, Asian art, Eastern literature, history of the Middle East, non-European government, and non-Western music.

The general education credit requirements for the AA and AS degrees are as follows:

	AA Degree	*AS Degree*
Communications	9 hours	9 hours
Humanities	9–13 hours (2 disciplines)	6–9 hours (2 disciplines)
Social sciences	9 hours (2 disciplines)	6 hours (2 disciplines)
Quantitative studies	6 hours	8 hours
Natural sciences	6 hours	8 hours
Non-Western studies	3 hours	3 hours

The general education credit requirements for the AAS degree are three hours in Communications and three hours in Quantitative studies.

The remaining courses must be selected from at least three of the four remaining categories. The general education component of the AAS degree may represent no less than 25 percent and no more than 50 percent of the total number of hours required for completion of a particular curriculum. For example, if sixty hours are required to complete a degree program, then fifteen to thirty credit hours may be general education courses.

History of General Education

General education at Black Hawk College has moved through three distinct phases of development in its fifty-year history: a hidden curriculum stage, a proliferation period, and, currently, a time of analysis. Between 1946 and 1962, the college did not identify distinct general education requirements but did, in fact, include a common core of English, speech, and other general education courses in all curricula. During this period, the college was offering programs of study modeled after various senior colleges and universities. General education was more of an implicit, hidden curriculum.

The second period began in 1962 when the college became an independent entity and was chartered as a comprehensive community college. At this time, the college published graduation requirements for only the AA and AS degrees. The general education component consisted of a core of three courses in communications and one in health science. In addition, students were required to choose six hours each from humanities, social sciences, and natural sciences distribution groups. Between 1962 and 1982, group A (humanities) increased 51 percent to include 100 courses. Group B (social sciences) grew 34 percent to include 62 courses, and group C (natural sciences) grew 29 percent to include 62 courses. This proliferation became even greater in 1977 with the addition of group D (human well-being) with its own 48 courses. Almost all transfer courses were included in the groupings as general education courses.

An ad hoc Curriculum Committee, appointed in 1980 to review the AA/AS degrees, questioned whether it was sound academic policy to allow students such a cafeteria-style menu of general education requirements. Furthermore, the committee expressed alarm that these distribution groups were allowed to grow over the previous twenty-year period without any real analysis of the effect of unconstrained elective choices on student learning.

The third period was characterized by more analytical thinking about general education. In 1983 the ad hoc Curriculum Committee recommended the first of several degree-requirement revisions. The committee used the following criteria to eliminate more than two hundred courses from the distribution selections.

Every general education course must:

- Be an introductory survey or appreciation course
- Be designed to meet the needs and interests of any student regardless of the student's area of emphasis

- Be offered on a regular basis
- Have no prerequisites

This first of several reductions in the distribution groups slashed the humanities group to fourteen courses, the social sciences to seventeen, the natural sciences to twenty-two, and human well-being to five courses. Not all changes resulted in the elimination of courses; one deficiency in the Associate in Arts degree was addressed by adding a mathematics, logic, or computer-literacy requirement to the core. Motivations for the drastic reduction included fiscal concerns, such as cutting the costs of staffing a large menu of courses, providing a varied curriculum while assuring sufficient enrollment, and reducing competition between introductory courses and applied majors courses.

Additional reasons for eliminating courses arose from concerns regarding the quality of course offerings and because of the need for simplicity of advising and articulation. An accreditation visit by the North Central Association (NCA) in 1986 further stimulated analysis of the general education curriculum. The visiting team found some AAS programs out of compliance with NCA requirements. Its evaluations led to the following events: a focus visit scheduled for 1989 to assure that general education course work had been incorporated into career programs; the development of a district general education policy statement; and the formation of the District Degree Committee.

This committee realigned the general education component of all degrees to conform with the requirements of the NCA as well as the Illinois Community College Board (ICCB). The Degree Committee developed the following definition of general education for Black Hawk College: "General education is a part of every student's formal course of study regardless of his/her technical, vocational or professional preparation; it is intended to provide lifelong learning, develop personal values, prepare individuals to adapt to change in an interdependent world community, foster self-esteem and motivation, and to attain skills in analysis, communication, quantification and synthesis" (Internal Degree Committee Document). In addition, this committee reaffirmed the four previously cited criteria that describe general education courses. Today, the Degree Committee's principal function is to monitor the shape of the general education curriculum and make changes when appropriate. The committee meets regularly to consider requests from departments to add courses to or delete them from the discipline distribution list.

In addition to the three historical periods of internal evolution, several external factors played and continue to play a role in molding the general education curriculum. In the past, the college had been free to set its own general education requirements so long as those requirements meet articulation agreements with four-year institutions. However, since 1988, when ICCB issued model AA and AS degree guidelines, the college has had less autonomy in specifying the general education curriculum. By 1994, all Illinois community colleges had chosen to conform to these models to ensure transferability to institutions.

Another powerful force shaping the general education curriculum at Black Hawk College is the accrediting agency for the college, the NCA. Each institution accredited by the NCA must demonstrate that it satisfies certain General Institution Requirements (GIRs) that the NCA uses to define the kind of institution it accredits. These GIRs include the requirement that general education be a component of undergraduate degree programs, as well as certificate and diploma programs of two or more academic years in length. In addition, as mentioned earlier, an NCA accreditation visit in 1986 served as a catalyst to further the analysis of the general education curriculum.

Other external agencies that affect general education requirements at Black Hawk College include the Illinois Board of Higher Education with its push for accountability, advisory committees with their input on occupational requirements, and admission requirements of senior institutions with whom Black Hawk has cooperative articulation agreements.

As is evident, substantial internal and external forces have molded general education at Black Hawk College. The role of the college community over the years has been to define the nature and philosophy of the curriculum. The role of external agencies has been to dictate its articulation and accountability.

Defining General Education Outcomes

The Degree Committee had established the theoretical foundation for general education at the college, but theory was not enough. It took the challenge of accountability to move theory into classroom practice. It is not surprising that the Outcomes Assessment Committee was responsible for focusing departmental attention on general education curriculum in practice. In an attempt to define operationally the outcomes of general education through a DACUM (Design A CUrriculuM) workshop, departments became more deeply involved with pedagogy and specifying learning objectives.

DACUM is a structured, group, consensus-seeking process that leads to the creation of a matrix of learning competencies (Norton, 1985). It was originally designed for the Job Corps in Clinton, Iowa, in the late 1960s as a tool in occupational analysis. Typical DACUM workshops include a panel of "expert workers" and a facilitator trained in the DACUM protocol. The facilitator is the process expert; the panel members are the content experts. The facilitator provides participants with rules for discussion, suggestions for etiquette, and guidance through the process. Through group consensus the panel determines broad functional areas of general responsibility called duties and the corresponding work activities called job tasks. These tasks accomplish duties and lead to a product, service, or decision. A DACUM is both a process and a product: the process is the actual workshop experience, while the product is the "chart" of learning objectives that the panel produces.

Black Hawk used a modified DACUM in July 1992 to specify student learning outcomes for the general education curriculum. In this case, seven faculty members and four administrators were the "expert workers." To reflect accomplishment from the student's perspective, the panel identified broad categories of *student abilities,* rather than duties, and corresponding *outcomes,* rather than job tasks. The facilitator instructed the panel to use the definition of general education developed by the Degree Committee, the current listing of general education courses, and the criteria the Degree Committee had used to select these courses in order to assist them in the development of the student abilities and the corresponding outcomes. The panel identified a range of abilities and corresponding measurable outcomes that students should possess upon completion of the general education requirements. Then it arranged the abilities and outcomes into a matrix (Table 1.1).

In an attempt to use the DACUM to measure general education outcomes, the Assessment Committee asked each department to evaluate general education courses. Faculty members identified outcomes listed in the matrix that were also outcomes or objectives in their course(s) and indicated how student attainment of these objectives could be measured. For example, one of the outcomes identified for Biology 145, Anatomy, and Physiology I, is the ability to convey ideas and information through writing. The instructor measures this outcome in two ways: as essay responses to questions on each unit exam and as critical analyses of journal articles related to course content.

These analyses are graded on both content and writing skills. After all faculty members had completed the identification of outcomes, the Assessment Committee gathered the information from both campuses and compared it to the matrix. The committee was relieved to find that each of the DACUM outcomes is taught in at least one general education course. However, whether a given student achieves an acceptable range of general education outcomes is the crucial, if still unanswered, question.

The DACUM moved Black Hawk's general education theory into practice in several ways. The chart serves as a tool for assessing the scope of the general education curriculum. And faculty now have a way to gather information about general education courses in order to implement improvements in the teaching/learning process. The Outcomes Assessment Committee has included the DACUM matrix as one of the assessment tools in the institutional plan for student academic achievement.

Lessons Learned

What has the institution learned from this experience? It is now obvious that more open communication, broader participation, and more timely feedback within the college community would enhance general education efforts at Black Hawk College. Given the college's information-overload environment, the committees probably should have designed a marketing campaign to reach strategically appropriate audiences with their findings and recommendations.

Achieving maximum college involvement is a prerequisite for success in curricular reform. The membership of the key committees must be representative of transfer and career faculty. It is important that the various constituents

Table 1.1. DACUM Matrix of Curriculum Outcomes

A Black Hawk college student completing the general education requirements will be able to:

Abilities

A. Apply Thinking Skills	B. Apply Quantitative Skills	C. Apply Communication Skills	D. Learn Throughout Life	E. Adapt to Change	F. Enhance Personal Values
A1. Use inductive and deductive reasoning.	B1. Utilize basic computational methods.	C1. Process information through listening.	D1. Recognize the value of learning.	E1. Recognize the process of change.	F1. Participate as a team member.
A2. Apply information.	B2. Utilize models to predict outcomes.	C2. Convey ideas and information through speaking.	D2. Demonstrate a positive attitude.	E2. Recognize interdependence of the World Community.	F2. Demonstrate self-esteem.
A3. Synthesize information.	B3. Interpret numerical data.	C3. Interpret written communication.	D3. Access information resources.	E3. Exhibit flexible thinking.	F3. Demonstrate motivation.
A4. Analyze information.	B4. Use experimental methods.	C4. Use standard English.	D4. Apply different learning techniques.	E4. Practice a proactive approach.	F4. Manage personal resources.
A5. Evaluate information.	B5. Demonstrate measurement techniques.	C5. Convey ideas and information through writing.	D5. Demonstrate a broad base of knowledge.	E5. Make decisions.	F5. Appreciate cultural diversity.
A6. Use problem-solving process.	B6. Generate visual representation of data.	C6. Adapt information flow to audience.	D6. Integrate new and existing knowledge.	E6. Take risks.	F6. Recognize environmental issues.
A7. Generate new ideas.	B7. Recognize limitations of quantitative data.	C7. Use alternative methods of communication.	D7. Exhibit a long-term perspective.	E7. Modify behaviors and attitudes.	F7. Demonstrate scientific, cultural, and technical literacy.
		C8. Use communication technology.		E8. Adapt to technological changes.	F8. Demonstrate work ethic.
				E9. Adapt to cultural diversity.	F9. Formulate a code of ethics.
					F10. Establish personal goals.

Outcomes

own the decision-making process. When a project as large as curricular reform is going to be undertaken, enough human and financial resources must be committed to complete the task. Released time for administrators and faculty, adequate clerical support staff, travel expenses, and staff development are imperative to achieve a high-quality product.

Questions

Many more questions than answers have arisen as a result of this experience with general education curricular reform. Following are just a few.

1. Is general education at Black Hawk College a curriculum or just a collection of disjointed courses? The faculty needs to pursue this question continuously through the Degree Committee. If it is truly a curriculum, then faculty must communicate with one another to better coordinate learning.

2. Should students enjoy complete freedom to design their general education curriculum, or should faculty steer them toward a preferred sequence? Should a student majoring in science choose different courses from a student majoring in English? If some majors, such as occupational (AAS) programs, require only the minimum of general education courses, then which ones should students take? None of these questions are easy to answer because they all impinge on competing departmental, discipline, or program interests.

3. Are students experiencing unnecessary duplication or gaps in their general education curriculum? To answer this question, the college needs a process for tracking students throughout their programs of study.

4. Should the responsibility for providing general education be evenly distributed throughout the college, or should it be the exclusive responsibility of only a few departments? Surely, students would benefit if an outcome such as conveying information through writing were taught across the curriculum and not just in English classes.

Although Black Hawk College has always been committed to general education, the college is just beginning to communicate the goals of general education to the students, measure progress toward those goals, and provide feedback to ensure student success.

References

Norton, R. E. *DACUM Handbook*. Leadership Training Series, no. 67. Columbus: National Center for Research in Vocational Education, Ohio State University, 1985.

DOROTHY R. MARTIN is director of the Teaching/Learning Center, past chair of the Degree Committee, current chair of the Outcomes Assessment Committee, and professor of biology at Black Hawk College.

SHEILA LILLIS is the assistant to the vice president for academic affairs at Black Hawk College.

In New York State, community colleges have considerable freedom
in framing their own general education program. After eight years
of debate and a full campus vote, Broome Community College
adopted a program incorporating core requirements and course
infusion focusing on seven key areas.

General Education at Broome Community College: Coherence and Purpose

Richard M. Romano

Broome Community College (BCC) is a unit of the State University of New York, located in south central New York State about two hundred miles from New York City. The college has one campus with approximately 6,500 (4,500 FTEs) students enrolled in credit courses, 75 percent of whom come from Broome County. The college is located in a suburban setting outside the city limits of Binghamton, the largest city (55,000) in a county (Broome) of approximately 220,000 people. The predominantly white student population (94 percent) reflects the racial and ethnic mix of the local community. The community also houses another unit of the State University, Binghamton University, which is a highly selective college of 12,000 students offering programs through the doctoral level.

BCC was founded in 1946 as a technical college but added programs in liberal arts and business in the 1960s. The college prides itself on the quality of its technical programs, which serve such local industries as IBM and Martin Marietta. However, these technical programs have suffered declining enrollments over the past ten years, and now approximately 50 percent of the student population is enrolled in liberal arts transfer programs. Academically, the college is divided into four divisions: Liberal Arts, Business and Office Technologies, Health Sciences, and Technologies and Computing. Its thirty-two degree programs have attracted approximately 30 percent of the local high school graduating class for the last twenty-five years. It graduated 1,070 students in 1993.

General Education Prior to 1987

The college offers AA, AS, and AAS degrees. The state of New York requires that these degree programs contain a certain distribution of general education courses (referred to as the liberal arts core), and it indicates that this core shall not be directed toward specialized study or specific occupational or professional objectives. The AAS programs in technical/occupational areas must contain at least one-third of their credits (twenty) in liberal arts subjects. The state suggests that these twenty credits be balanced among the humanities, social sciences, and math/sciences areas, but it is left to each campus to decide what this balance will be. The BCC campus has no overall curriculum committee, and substantial power for setting degree requirements rests with the faculty of each degree program.

At BCC we have traditionally required all degree students to take a minimum of six credits in English (usually two composition courses), six credits in social science (free choice among fifty-four different courses), and six to eight credits in math/science. Most AAS and all AA and AS programs exceeded this minimum, but the distribution requirements remained substantially unchanged in the twenty-five years prior to the new 1987 general education reform. There was some rationale for the established distribution requirements, such as exposing students to diverse modes of inquiry, but for the most part the requirements simply represented a political compromise among the departments involved.

Process and Rationale for Reform

The movement at the college to reexamine what became known as the general education core was initiated by the liberal arts faculty. It came at a time, in the late 1970s, when the country was experiencing a new wave of interest in curriculum reform. Following the publication of Harvard's *Report on the Core Curriculum* in 1978, the dean of the Liberal Arts Division urged his chairs to read it. Following this, a small core of faculty within that division began to read the relevant literature, most notably Boyer and Levine's *A Quest for Common Learning* (1980), and study the new programs at Miami-Dade in Florida (Lukenbill and McCabe, 1978), and Los Medanos (*Los Medanos College,* 1976) in California, among others.

During this early period, some liberal arts faculty came to believe that the general education program at the college had been vocationalized too much. In technical programs, faculty counseled students into general education courses that were closer to vocational objectives. For instance, in some AAS programs, faculty succeeded in substituting Technical Writing for more liberally educative humanities courses. Of course, vocational and general education goals were not always incompatible, and vocationally oriented course selections seemed to make sense given the community college mission. Nevertheless, as the national movement for reform gained momentum, a growing

number of faculty began to feel that the general education distribution requirements at BCC lacked intellectual coherence and reflected no clear educational
purpose.

During the 1980–81 academic year, the Liberal Arts Division began a
lengthy discourse on general education. By 1983, the division had produced
a proposal, debated its features, and amended and approved it. This was, in
effect, the Liberal Arts General Education plan.

Upon the request of the liberal arts faculty, the vice president for Academic
Affairs initiated a campuswide discussion of general education based on the liberal arts plan. From this point on, a task force and a variety of committees
examined the various aspects of the plan, and a campuswide General Education Steering Committee was appointed to guide the process. An implementation plan was presented to the entire faculty in 1986 and was passed by full vote
of teaching and nonteaching professionals at the college. Full implementation
of the plan began with the freshman class in the fall semester, 1987. The final
product reflected the feeling that the existing distribution requirements were
not adequately addressing the following learning deficiencies:

- Poor communication skills (writing and speaking)
- Lack of sophisticated reasoning abilities
- Lack of ethical awareness and inexperience with moral reasoning
- Inadequate understanding of science and technology for effective citizenship
- Lack of empathetic understanding of racial, ethnic, and cultural differences
- Insufficient understanding of the obligations of democratic citizenship and
  the means of effective political participation
- Inadequately developed commitments to physical and mental health and
  fitness

This catalogue of learning deficiencies provided the rationale for general
education reform at the college.

The Plan

The General Education Steering Committee established seven subcommittees
to study each of the seven areas previously cited. The subcommittees were
Effective Communication, Moral Reasoning, Civic Education/Public Affairs,
Critical Thinking, Global/Intercultural Perspectives, Technological Literacy, and
Health and Fitness. An additional subcommittee on the "extracurriculum" was
charged with developing campuswide activities, such as lectures and extracurricular activities, that advanced the overall goals of general education on campus. Each of the eight subcommittees issued a report, which was published in
a shortened form in campus publications. This gave faculty a chance to react
to what was being planned and it also helped prepare the way for a campus
vote on the overall proposal.

The final plan moved the college away from the view that general education meant fulfilling distribution requirements in the conventional liberal arts

academic categories—science and mathematics, social sciences, and humanities. Instead, the faculty set about to define the knowledge, skills, abilities, personal attributes, and dispositions that they believed every graduate ought to acquire. These general education goals were broadly conceived rather than technically narrow, with the overriding concern of developing the associated competencies required of an educated citizenry. Once these goals were agreed upon, faculty would be expected to incorporate them into their courses and curricula.

The general education requirements of the college are published in the college catalogue and are presented to students in a plainly written pamphlet entitled *A Common Learning: General Education at Broome Community College* (1994). This ten-page pamphlet is distributed to all students during the orientation process. The pamphlet contains the following statement concerning the goals of general education at the college: "The General Education Program at Broome Community College aims to equip graduates with the skills, knowledge, and sensibilities which they will need to function effectively in a complex, interdependent world. These learning goals are also intended to advance our societal well-being by strengthening our social and civic bonds. General education complements technical and occupational education by nurturing critical and creative qualities of the mind and disposition, and also by addressing the public domain of education where questions of the collective good and of social obligation and justice are raised" (p.1).

The curricular design used to advance these goals can be divided into two parts: a required core program and a voluntary course infusion program. The first part of the plan called for incorporating general education goals into a "core" of courses through which all students in the college would pass. Certain required courses were designated as either primary or secondary carriers of the seven different aspects of the general education program. Through a painfully long process, each degree program at the college was modified to include the required core. In addition, departments were encouraged to develop their own courses—curriculum-based writing courses, for example—that would satisfy some of these requirements. All courses designated as core courses needed the approval of the General Education Steering Committee, which took on the role as the "keeper of the core." This core program was not voluntary and could not be bypassed by students who wanted a degree from the college.

The second part of the plan was to infuse as many courses as possible with content and methodologies responsive to the generic general education goals. Thus we had "writing across the curriculum," "moral reasoning across the curriculum," and so on. This aspect of the plan was voluntary, but the eight general education committees organized workshops and the college offered financial incentives for faculty who wanted to infuse these objectives into their courses. The writing across the campus effort was merged with a similar effort going on independently within the English department at the time and has had the largest impact on the curriculum, to date, of all the infusion efforts.

The Requirements

The key features of the new general education program are summarized below. In each case a brief definition of the generic requirement is given, as well as how it is to be met. This is followed by a statement concerning the assessment of that goal. These seven goals apply to all students at the college and represent the minimum requirements for the AAS degree. (Students enrolled in AA and AS transfer programs must meet additional distribution requirements in the arts and sciences for their degrees. For instance, most transfer students are studying for the AA degree, which requires a full year each of history, literature, and philosophy or foreign language.)

Requirement No. 1: Communicating Effectively. Communicating effectively means sharing thoughts and feelings with others in speaking and in writing and, as a consequence, influencing their thinking.

Each student at the college takes ENG 110, Written Expression, which is a basic composition course. The course is usually taken in the first semester at the college and must be preceded by developmental courses if placement test scores are low. This is much the same as the prereform requirement. The second English course, however, was moved from the second semester to the end of the student's degree program. In between, students are required to take two "W" (writing) emphasis courses. These courses are offered by faculty in all four divisions at the college, and most students outside the liberal arts area are now getting at least one of these "W" courses from their occupational or preprofessional courses. Ideally, in their last semester of work, students take the second English/Humanities course, entitled Communicating About Ideas and Values (ENG 220). As the title implies, this new capstone course, designed by the English faculty, serves as a final assessment of writing and speaking skills and carries primary responsibility for helping students acquire facility with moral reasoning, critical thinking, and cross-cultural inquiry.

In summary, the sequence goes as follows: ENG 110→"W"→"W"→ENG 220. The class quota for all "W" courses was dropped from the normal thirty-five to twenty-five, with the added suggestion that no person should teach more than three of these sections per semester. The normal teaching load is five courses. Preliminary assessment indicates that this writing program is stronger and more coherent than the previous one. Students note that the college is serious about writing, because it is required in courses throughout their program and faculty outside the English department assume greater responsibility for writing instruction. The English department has experimented with portfolio assessment, but to date lack of funding has kept the college from fully implementing it.

Requirement No. 2: Acting Civically. Effective citizenship consists of the capability to participate actively and intelligently in public affairs.

Prior to reform, education for civic competence was not a part of any degree program. All students were required to take two social science courses, and liberal arts students had an additional two-course history requirement.

These distribution requirements are still in place after reform, but now one of the social science courses must be selected from a list of seven courses that are strongly oriented toward civic education. The requirement in civic education narrows the students' choice of courses and concentrates the efforts of the faculty on a select group of courses attuned to the specific goals of general education. The designated civic education core courses are: Public Affairs (SOS 111), Social Problems (SOC 111), Science, Technology, and Society (SOS 120), Macroeconomics (ECO 111), Introduction to American Government (POS 201), American State and Local Government (POS 204), and U.S. History I (HIS 130).

The overriding purpose of these courses is to assist students in participating actively and intelligently in public affairs. All of the seven core courses give students practice in confronting public policy issues, understanding and interpreting our important civic documents, analyzing issues historically, and applying the ethical content of key democratic concepts like justice, equality, tolerance, freedom, and responsibility to public problems.

Assessment techniques, beyond classroom evaluation, have not been implemented. The subcommittee is currently developing an inventory of assessable learning activities.

Requirement No. 3: Thinking Globally and Cross-Culturally. A global (international and cross-cultural) perspective includes at least three aspects. First is development of a cross-cultural awareness and perspective. Second is a "state of the planet" awareness, and third is a knowledge of global dynamics.

Prior to reform, this goal was not a part of the general education requirement. Now, the seven civic education core courses mentioned earlier must also consider global or intercultural perspectives. As a general rule at least 20 percent of the course work must be so directed. In addition, the required core course in English/Humanities (ENG 220) must include expository and literary works from different cultural perspectives. Course and curriculum infusion of this goal has been embraced by the faculty, and the college has also made a determined effort to internationalize the campus by recruiting foreign students (100 to 150 a semester) and providing overseas study programs for students and travel opportunities for faculty. Assessment of this goal is incomplete. A global awareness test is being considered.

Requirement No. 4: Thinking Critically. Critical thinking is the capacity to think rationally and reflectively about an issue or argument and to reach sound judgments based upon evidence and good reasoning. A critical thinker will strive for clarity of expression, logical consistency, and impartiality in interpreting all pertinent facts. A true critical thinker is also motivated by intellectual honesty and appreciative sympathy with the convictions of others.

Prior to reform, critical thinking was not a clearly defined goal, although it was implicitly assumed to be the primary goal of the educational process. Under the new general education plan faculty were asked to consciously incorporate critical thinking techniques into their instructional methods. Core courses in English (ENG 110 and ENG 220), civic education, and math and science were expected to bear principal responsibility for critical thinking pedagogy, but many other faculty have also embraced the effort. The critical thinking subcommittee organized activities to promote faculty awareness of how to infuse aspects of critical thinking into all courses.

Limited attempts have been made to assess this goal. Some instructors have experimented with the Watson-Glazer test, but the results have been inconclusive. Sometime in the future we plan to conduct a longitudinal assessment of critical thinking development.

Requirement No. 5: Reasoning Ethically. Moral reasoning and evaluation is the process of trying to distinguish right from wrong and then choosing and justifying one's decision. To achieve competence in moral argument, one should be able to explain to others why one judges something right or wrong relative to an alternative judgment.

Prior to reform, no systematic attempt was made to include this as a general education goal. Now, faculty teaching the core course Communicating About Ideas and Values, ENG 220, are required to engage students in moral discourse on course readings. The six core courses in civic education explore public policy issues relating to justice and fairness. Evaluation of student progress in moral reasoning is mainly classroom based, although an expanded writing portfolio program could be part of a longitudinal assessment in the future.

Requirement No. 6: Understanding and Using Math, Science, and Technology. Mathematical literacy, or "numeracy," is the ability to deal with the fundamental notions of number and chance. Scientific literacy includes an understanding of key concepts and principles of science; a familiarity with the natural world and recognition of both its diversity and unity; and an ability to use scientific knowledge and scientific ways of thinking for individual and social purposes.

Technology is the means through which mathematical and scientific knowledge is applied to solving problems in fields such as transportation, communication, medicine, food production, and environmental management. It also implies that one is able to reason critically about the impact of innovative technology upon the individual and society. To participate effectively in civic life, one must have knowledge of mathematics, science, and technology in order to make well-reasoned judgments on the uses of pertinent techniques and information.

Prior to reform, all programs required at least two courses in science and mathematics; this requirement still stands, and faculty are newly committed to integrating computing into their courses, where feasible. Required course work in civic education, as well as the college's co-curricular programming, supports and reinforces this objective. Assessment of student understanding beyond classroom evaluation has not been discussed.

Requirement No. 7: Maintaining Good Health and Fitness. Good health and physical fitness are key elements of what has come to be called wellness. Wellness is a physical and emotional state of feeling fit: of being able to participate fully and productively in work, study, and recreational activity, and to possess the reserves of strength and energy to accomplish extraordinary tasks.

To date this has been a requirement for students in transfer programs. A fitness profile test is administered to all students in designated physical education (PED) classes. They are provided with an individual program of activity designed to improve or maintain their health and fitness. Students in transfer programs take a minimum of one (1) credit of designated cardiovascular-intensive physical education, and all others are encouraged to enroll in PED courses, or to use the college's exercise facilities.

Making Connections Through the Extracurriculum

The extracurriculum component of general education offers students opportunities outside the classroom to participate in a rich array of planned activities such as convocations, public forums, conferences, and performing arts events. Public affairs programs aim at connecting classroom learning with current events. They demonstrate the relevance of the general education program and help students grasp the important relationships between their studies and the range of vexing problems that confront us in the world, the nation, and in our communities. Performance activities, on the other hand, aim at widening and deepening students' understanding of and appreciation for the arts of creative expression.

Each year the Extracurriculum Committee, in consultation with the campus community, establishes a convocation theme that serves to focus the various forums and symposia scheduled throughout the fall and spring semesters. Faculty and students from the college's four academic divisions and Student Affairs are involved. Extracurricular programs support and reinforce the various goals of the general education program, in particular, civic education, critical and moral reasoning and judgment, global/multicultural perspective, and scientific and technological "literacy."

Over the past several years, specific activities have included prominent national and international speakers addressing such themes as cultural unity and diversity, the ecological crisis, the computer industry in transition, nuclear arms control, discovery and creativity, and the global population crisis; conferences on such topics as Black Literature, Working Class Literature, and Homelessness; public forums on the Gulf Crisis and the subsequent Gulf War; and dramatic presentations and dance. These programs enable students, faculty, and staff to experience a unique form of intellectual and emotional engagement as a "community of learners."

A Final Note on Assessment

In 1991 the college was required to submit a campuswide assessment plan to the State University of New York, which included general education. Because our general education requirements were somewhat unique to our campus, assessment became a particularly complicated task, since standardized packages, such as those offered by American College Testing Service (ACT), were not completely congruent with what we were trying to measure.

The General Education Steering Committee has defined assessment in terms of student learning outcomes, while recognizing that to date the general education program of the college has been preoccupied with curriculum and course design. We have some control over these inputs and can monitor whether the faculty are carrying out the design of the general education plan. However, we realize that the real test of assessment is to measure the impact on the students.

Techniques currently in use include surveys of graduates, transfer institutions, and employers. Additional assessment techniques under consideration include alumni interviews, student portfolios, standardized pre- and post-course exams, library statistics on utilization and other such "trace" data, final projects for students, and common exit exams in selected courses.

We are still struggling with this process and have made some attempts at both quantitative and qualitative assessment of most of the goals. However, the major topic of discussion within the General Education Steering Committee these days is the assessment issue, and we will not know whether our overall program is having the desired effect until a comprehensive program is in place.

What we have found, however, is that our discussion of assessment has led us into a discussion of classroom teaching techniques and pedagogies that promote more interaction between faculty and students. A rethinking of our delivery system promises to contribute in a positive way to our desired outcomes.

Lessons Learned

At Broome Community College we have learned that curriculum changes cannot be adopted wholesale from some other campus. That does not mean that we cannot learn from the experience of others but only that each campus has its own culture, institutional governance, and statewide regulations that regulate the approach and final product. Based on our experience, the following bits of advice seem warranted:

1. Be patient! Changing a curriculum takes years.
2. Pay close attention to the degree requirements for general or liberal education mandated by your state.
3. Start with a small group of dedicated faculty. Do not move beyond this group until you all understand the purpose that you have in mind. Gradually spread your net to include faculty from all areas of the college.
4. Do not count on administrative help for leadership in this area. Build momentum among the faculty and work to bring the administration around to your way of thinking.
5. Design a program that makes sense for your campus. Study other models and their rationales and adapt them to fit the culture of your college.

6. Appoint a campuswide general education committee that can guide the development and implementation of the plan. Make it a permanent committee with rotating membership once the plan is institutionalized.
7. Be flexible! Compromise! Provide a mechanism for modifying and updating the plan. Encourage faculty to submit courses or methods that will help students meet the requirements.
8. Get your college to devote resources, such as grants and faculty sabbatical leaves, toward accomplishing the goals of the plan.

Clearly, the process of change will be difficult at any campus. Just as clearly, however, that process has a number of positive institutional benefits, including faculty renewal and the development of a greater sense of community. The dialogue generated during and after the reform process at BCC enriched both the faculty and the students involved. Indeed, it is the process itself that may have generated the most lasting benefits to the college, and it is ongoing.

References

A Common Learning: General Education at Broome Community College. Binghamton, N.Y.: Broome Community College, 1994.

Boyer, E., and Levine, A. *Quest for Common Learning.* Washington, D.C.: The Carnegie Foundation for the Advancement of Teaching, 1981.

Harvard Committee. *Report on the Core Curriculum.*Cambridge, Mass: Office of the Dean, Faculty of Arts and Sciences, Harvard University, 1978.

Los Medanos College: The Education Plan. Pittsburg, Calif.: Community College Press, 1976.

Lukenbill, J. D., and McCabe, R. H. *General Education in a Changing Society.* Dubuque, IA: Kendall/Hunt, 1978.

RICHARD M. ROMANO is professor of economics at Broome Community College. He has been a member of the General Education Steering Committee since its inception in 1985.

General education serves the Bunker Hill Community College learning community as an academic commons where students from diversely rich cultural and linguistic backgrounds can come together and share common intellectual experiences.

Bunker Hill Community College: A Common Experience for Lifelong Learning

Malinda M. Smutek

Founded in 1973, Bunker Hill Community College (BHCC) is a comprehensive, public, urban institution located in Boston's historic Charlestown. With its Chelsea Campus, Bunker Hill Community College serves the Commonwealth of Massachusetts as one of fifteen community colleges. Bunker Hill has five academic divisions: Allied Health Sciences, Communication, Liberal Arts and Sciences, Public and Community Service, and Technology. It offers more than seventy associate degree and certificate programs.

Bunker Hill provides high-quality, affordable education to about 6,500 day and evening students who constitute a student population that is ethnically, racially, and linguistically diverse. The average age of the students in the day program is twenty-eight, and thirty-three in the evening program. The ethnic composition of BHCC's student body consists of African American, Hispanic, Asian, Native American, and white students. More than 45 percent of the students are of color. Representative native languages include Russian, Polish, Spanish, Italian, Portuguese, Vietnamese, Khmer, Chinese, Japanese, Korean, Haitian French, French, Yiddish, and English. The international (visa) students and refugee students who study each semester come from more than sixty-six countries. Bunker Hill has one of the largest English as a Second Language programs in New England. The college offers a variety of programs to meet the needs of students who plan to transfer to a four-year college or university; who want to prepare for immediate employment; who study at the college level for career advancement or personal enrichment; and/or who return for job retraining. More than 10 percent of the students attending Bunker Hill have advanced degrees.

NEW DIRECTIONS FOR COMMUNITY COLLEGES, no. 92, Winter 1995   © Jossey-Bass Publishers

Institutional Aims of General Education

Bunker Hill is committed to creating a learning environment in which students' potentials can be developed. While potential is difficult to assess, there can be little argument that it continues to develop long after the student has graduated from, or left, Bunker Hill. The college's general education curriculum, included in every Associate in Arts and Associate in Science degree-granting program, provides a basis for a commitment to lifelong learning. General education makes available to all students a wide variety of courses that add breadth to each student's store of knowledge and introduce students to essential aspects of global and American cultures.

Bunker Hill recognizes that there are things all human beings share, and it has implemented a general education curriculum that acknowledges those commonalities. Boyer and Levine (1981), for example, maintain that general education's mission is to reaffirm the connectedness among all individuals. It is an educational concept that supports "a curricular acknowledgement that individualism alone is insufficient" (Levine, 1990, p. 51). Its agenda is the development and integration of "every student's knowledge, skills, attitudes, and experiences so that the student can engage effectively in a lifelong process of inquiry and decision making" (Lukenbill and McCabe, 1978, p. 29).

Some might argue that Bunker Hill's comprehensive general education curriculum burdens students who choose a career track option and seek only to acquire workplace skills. The general education curriculum, however, aims to provide to all students the intellectual flexibility and knowledge to support lifelong learning. Also, many occupational program students may at some time decide to continue their education. In today's rapidly changing society and economy, narrow job skills quickly become obsolete. Consequently, knowledge of the principles that enable mastery of new technologies and techniques, which underlie the ability to use human relations skills at work and which facilitate the adaptation to changing job placements, will serve the student for many years in this lifelong learning process (Bartkovich, 1981).

Although sensitive to the needs and realities of its students, Bunker Hill strives to provide them opportunities to be "removed from the daily activities and anxieties associated with earning a living in order to understand and reflect upon those permanent or universal concepts which have shaped civilization and (which) will shape them decades to come" (Lukenbill and McCabe, 1978, p. 54). Its general education curriculum is the locus of lifelong learning skills and values, as well as the knowledge and understanding essential to whatever future roles students might choose.

General Education Goals

Bunker Hill's dynamic curriculum aims to be responsive to the cultural, economic, educational, linguistic, political, societal, and technological forces that constantly affect the student and community. As Miller (1988) pointed out in

The Meaning of General Education, the technological revolution has moved much faster than our economic, political, and social institutions' abilities to adapt: it is not only technology that is changing, "it is the intricate fabric of society, the collection and organization of shared assumptions and principles that are the common stock of thought and action in daily life, that are only too quickly being transformed" (p. 1).

Given that the mission of Bunker Hill is defined by the needs of the student and the community, the function of its general education curriculum is to enable students to better understand and meet the challenges of a changing world (Gaff, 1983). Bunker Hill believes that the college experience should and must address the whole person, and it envisions that general education's integration of lifelong learning skills into each degree granting program of study will provide the foundation for a fuller life. Specifically, it maintains that its general education curriculum will guide its students toward the successful attainment of the following nine goals:

Aesthetics. Students will explore the dimensions of cultural and creative expressions of the human intellect and imagination. They will learn how to incorporate the arts to enrich their lives.

Career. Students will develop those skills necessary for a productive professional life and will learn how to set educational goals and objectives for their individual professional pursuits.

Communication. Students will develop the ability to perceive, gather, organize, and present information by a variety of means, verbal and nonverbal alike. They will also learn how to apply such abilities to exploring interpersonal communication needs such as conflict resolution, problem solving, and negotiations.

Critical Thinking. Students will learn how to think analytically and reason logically using current information and past experience to make informed judgments and to exhibit practical application.

Earth, Life, and Technology. Students will investigate the laws, theories, and scientific methods of inquiry used to explain the physical universe, its life forms, and its natural phenomena. They will examine the applications of this knowledge that have produced technology. They will also study the impact of human behavior on the environment and the implications of such behavior for their lives.

Ethics and Values. Students will participate in the study of conduct (ethics) and the study of beliefs (values). They will examine the sources of their ethical system, the nature of their values, and the impact their ethics and values have on their quality of life.

Global Awareness. Students will examine the development and maintenance of cultural identity. They will study the role of cultural identity in a multicultural environment. They will also examine the interdependence of cultures. In addition, students will explore global survival issues, such as ecology, economics, education, food, government structures, health, natural resources development, and population growth.

Holistic Health. Students will identify and examine the major health issues of the day, explore their impact on the individual and society, and investigate methods of prevention and control. Students will also identify and examine their own major health requirements and lifestyles. They will set objectives for lifelong physical and emotional well-being.

Human Relations. Students will learn about human relationships and behavior within institutions through history and within and among diverse social, linguistic, and racial groups. They will learn how to apply this knowledge of human behavior to their development of human relations skills.

General Education Program: Core and Distribution

The nine general education goals detailed earlier are infused throughout the courses listed in the general education course menu. This curricular menu constitutes a general education program consisting of twenty-one to twenty-two credits made up of both core and distribution offerings and is required of all Associate in Arts and Associate in Science degree students. Six of these credits must include the "core" requirement of College Writing I and II. In addition, students must complete the equivalent of fifteen to sixteen credits in five general education "distribution" categories. Course choices within these five distribution groupings may be specified by students' individual programs of study. To ensure breadth among course selections, no more than one course from a single prefix may be used to complete distribution requirements. The core and distribution requirements are satisfied in the following way:

Core Requirement: Communications (6 credits). These courses seek to develop students' ability to perceive, gather, organize, and present information and ideas by a variety of means. Students must take College Writing I and II.

Distribution Requirement: Individual and Society (3 credits). These courses examine one of the fundamental issues we all face in our development, namely, the interrelationship of the individual and the community. The interactions of the individual with the family, the school or college, the corporation, the voluntary associations we form, and/or the government are studied. Emphasis is placed on how individuals shape and are shaped by institutions, belief systems, and conduct. Students must choose one course from the following: Principles of Psychology, Introduction to Philosophy, Introduction to Ethics, Principles of Sociology, and Cultural Anthropology.

Distribution Requirement: Modern Civilization (3 credits). In these courses students will study selected and timely issues of the modern global systems, such as ecology, economics, education, food, government structures, health, natural resources development, and population growth. Students will come to understand the global issues encountered in reconciling divergent views and resolving conflicts. Equally important, students will begin to develop their own perspectives with respect to global issues and the development and maintenance of cultural identity and its role in a multicultural environment. Students must choose one course from the following: Macroeconomics, Microeconomics,

History of Western Civilization II, World Civilization I and II, U.S. History II, World Regional Geography, and World Religions.

Distribution Requirement: Scientific View of the World (4 credits). These courses examine the fundamental similarity of all matter and life in the universe. The aim is to provide the basic elements of scientific and technological literacy. Students investigate the laws, theories, and scientific methods of inquiry used to explain the physical universe, its life forms, and its natural phenomena. They examine the applications of this knowledge that have produced technology. They also study the impact of human behavior on the environment and its relations to quality of life. Students must choose one laboratory-based science from the following: Environmental Science and Lab, Earth Science I and II and Lab, Principles of Biology I and II and Lab, General Biology I and Lab, General Physics I and Lab, College Physics I and Lab, Chemical Science I and Lab, and General Chemistry I and Lab.

Distribution Requirement: Creative Exploration (3 credits). In these courses students will study art, dance, film, music, literature, languages, and theater. Students learn how to view their world through the dynamics and syntax of diverse modes of expression. Students explore the dimensions of cultural, linguistic, and creative expressions of the human intellect and imagination and come to understand how they harmonize their personal visions with their cultural times. Students must choose one course from the humanities disciplines.

General Education Implementation

Bunker Hill used a collaborative decision-making model for its general education initiative. First, faculty and staff volunteered to serve on a General Education Task Force that set the parameters of the debate and research in 1989. From the task force came a core of faculty volunteers to form a General Education Curriculum Review Steering Committee. This committee was composed of seven AA and AS faculty members and one administrator. It elected a chairperson to facilitate its activities. The president released each faculty member of this Steering Committee from one course each semester for the duration of the project, from 1990 to 1994. During the summer, the president provided stipends for the Steering Committee faculty members.

The major initial task was the establishment of communication and feedback systems to ensure community participation. Town meetings were held each semester so that anyone could meet with the Steering Committee members and ask questions or give recommendations. Regularly scheduled meetings and workshops were conducted for department chairs and their departments during the four years. A general education network was created that assigned a Steering Committee member to a particular division and its departments. In addition, meetings were held with individual college community members at their request, and a general education newsletter was regularly published. Also, information concerning general education was placed in the student newspaper, faculty and staff newsletter, and local area newspapers.

A communication system was also implemented. The General Education Steering Committee distributed yearly reports to the college community. It passed out surveys and questionnaires to elicit responses to its reports. The Steering Committee published the responses without using the names of the respondents. Moreover, the Steering Committee published report revisions based on the comments of college community members. Likewise, the Steering Committee presented updates to the College Forum, Board of Trustees, President's Cabinet, Academic Deans, and Student Government. The Steering Committee invited guest speakers and trainers such as Arthur Levine, Jerry Gaff, and Terry O'Banion to the college for the benefit of the college community.

The process of verifying the incorporation of goals into the courses is the purview of the Curriculum Committee, using standardized forms developed by the General Education Steering Committee. This committee examined the syllabus of each of the courses and the curriculum of each of the programs of study. It also developed another series of standardized forms to enable departments to designate to the Curriculum Committee the current course status: existing course, existing course to be general-education modified, or a new course. In addition, the Steering Committee developed a process for the Curriculum Committee that requires a department to submit a catalogue description, a course syllabus, and the general education course objectives before a course can be considered for the general education distribution categories. Furthermore, each program of study must demonstrate to what extent, major or minor, each general education goal is met in each course. This general education goal grid is necessary in order to enable the college to present to accrediting agencies the extent of its general education compliance.

To demonstrate a relationship between the general education goals and course requirements, the General Education Steering Committee, working with the college community, delineated general education competencies and the method with which these competencies will be met. This is summarized in Table 3.1. Once the general education program was implemented in fall 1994, the work and charge of the General Education Steering Committee ended and a general education curriculum was in place. Thereafter, departments or individuals wishing to prepare courses for inclusion in the general education course menu would make their proposal submissions directly to the Curriculum Committee.

As is the case with any curriculum reform, Bunker Hill expects that the general education curriculum will undergo continuous fine-tuning in the coming years. There will always remain a constant need for review and oversight of the general education curriculum if Bunker Hill intends to accomplish the following goals:

- Ensure that all nine general education goals and the equivalent of twenty-one general education credits (six core areas) are infused throughout a program
- Allow programs flexibility in meeting general education requirements while satisfying liberal arts, transfer, and career accreditation requirements

- Provide a process for the liberal arts service departments to identify courses as meeting general education core requirements (menu courses)
- Provide a process for the liberal arts service departments to assign general education course equivalent credit for courses required by AS programs
- Identify a need to create new courses or modify existing courses to meet general education requirements
- Provide documentation for curriculum committee evaluation
- Provide documentation for institutional accreditation review

Bunker Hill Community College affirms the following as integral to achieving its general education goals: (1) any AA and AS student can take any course listed in the general education menu; and (2) instructors teaching general education courses will understand what general education objectives are to be taught and how they are to be presented. Alternative courses to the traditional classroom format, such as External Studies, Telecourses, and Contract Learning, should also incorporate the general education goals and competencies listed in the general education course menu.

For these premises to be valid, any course submitted to the Curriculum Committee for inclusion in a general education distribution category must be presented to the respective liberal arts and sciences departments for review. These liberal arts and sciences departments will be given the opportunity to make recommendations to the Curriculum Committee. The justification for this procedure is based on the understanding that general education is not meant to displace the liberal arts and sciences foundation of all programs of study as stipulated by the New England Association of Schools and Colleges (NEASC), which accredits Bunker Hill.

At this juncture, Bunker Hill has developed general education requirements and a general education course menu responsive to the following: (1) the NEASC mandate that all programs of study include twenty-one credits of liberal arts and sciences in each program of study and a minimum of twenty-one credits of general education (December 1991); (2) the Higher Education Coordinating Council, which in October 1991 reaffirmed the *Undergraduate Experience* report of the former board of regents mandating all community colleges to have a minimum of twenty credits of general education; (3) Career/Occupational Program faculty members who emphatically stated that they could not replace any of their concentration requirements with general education courses; and (4) the lack of substantiated data presented by the Associate in Science degree programs that demonstrate the transferability of career/occupational courses as liberal arts and sciences electives.

It is hoped that future dialogue among career/occupational faculty, NEASC officials, and area institutions that accept BHCC's transfer students will result in the inclusion of career/occupational courses in the general education course menu. Presently three AS programs have developed new courses for the general education distribution categories: American Legal Systems (Criminal Justice), Principles of International Business (Business Administration), and American

Table 3.1. General Education Goal/Core Competencies for the Associate in Arts and Associate in Science Degrees

Goals/Competencies	Implementation	Credits
Comprehensive Interrelated Skills Including: Ethics, Values, and Critical Thinking Identify a problem Define alternative solutions Evaluate alternative solutions Apply scientific reasoning Demonstrate systematic planning skills Apply time-management skills Function independently Apply ethical choices Evaluate personal values Apply the content and methodology from various disciplines to address an issue or problem	Core competencies should be introduced and progressively reinforced throughout a program. Specific attention should be given to stressing the Comprehensive Interrelated Skills. A program proposal should include reference to how the total curriculum helps develop the Comprehensive Interrelated Skills.	n/a
Communications Comprehend, analyze, and synthesize written material Express concepts in writing	All degree graduates must: A. Remediate any deficiencies indicated on the Comprehensive Placement Test (CPT) for reading and English B. Take ENG 111 and ENG 112	6
Mathematics Apply basic arithmetic skills Apply basic algebra skills Use mathematics systematically to evaluate and solve problems	All degree graduates must: A. Remediate any deficiencies indicated on the Comprehensive Placement Test (CPT) for mathematics B. Take at least three credits of math above the 100 level from Quantitative Thought category unless MAT 100 is allowed in program requirements	3
Holistic Health Understand lifelong value of physical fitness Practice physical fitness	The college shall make opportunities available for students to develop these competencies by means of activities sponsored by the Office of Student Development and Student Athletics and Activities.	0

Holistic Health (continued)
- Apply stress-management skills
- Understand nutrition
- Understand major health issues
- Understand value of lifelong emotional well-being

Computer
- Demonstrate basic knowledge and understanding of operation and use of computers
- Adapt to computer applications

0 — All degree graduates must demonstrate ability to use a computer. This can be achieved through
A. Credit or noncredit general computer skills experience course or
B. Credit by examination or work and life experience demonstrating computer application skills or
C. Program content course requiring significant application on a computer as a problem-solving tool.

Career
- Understand basic skills necessary for a productive professional life
- Learn how to set educational goals and objectives for individual professional pursuits

0 — The college shall make available opportunities for students to develop basic professional skills. Divisions and programs are encouraged to develop these competencies by integrating such competencies into courses or other supplemental services.

Aesthetics, Human Relations, and Global Awareness
- Understand basic economic principles
- Evaluate historical basis of current society
- Evaluate diversity of world cultures
- Evaluate societal structures and influences
- Evaluate the influences of the arts
- Understand the developmental processes that shape the individual

9 — All degree graduates must take at least three credits in each of the following categories: Creative Exploration, Individual and Society, or Modern Civilization.

Earth, Life, and Technology
- Recognize the value of natural and physical sciences
- Evaluate the function and impact of technology
- Investigate the laws, theories, and scientific methods of inquiry used to explain the physical universe

3/4 — All degree graduates must take three or four credits in the category called Scientific View of the World.

Studies and Culture (ESL). Faculty for these three courses believe that their courses are transferable and plan to supply the necessary verification of such transferability to the Curriculum Committee.

Once the career/occupational programs have some of their courses included in the general education menu, all AA and AS students will have the opportunity to take them, thereby increasing enrollment in these general education occupational courses. In addition, these programs will be able to free up at least three additional credits for use by their students as program concentration requirements.

Assessment

Bunker Hill Community College considers assessment essential for educational improvement. It endorses the need for systematically collecting, interpreting, and using information about student learning. Current assessment practice is defined as examining student achievement within courses and asking about cumulative learning outcomes (McClenney, 1993). Bunker Hill believes that assessment that examines student achievement and cumulative learning outcomes should lead to real improvement of the general education curriculum.

Three-Year Internal Monitoring Process. The general education curriculum is monitored by the dean of the division sponsoring general education courses. This evaluation process reviews classroom instruction, course syllabi, course materials, student achievement and retention in accordance with the Collective Bargaining Agreement. Students and Student Affairs staff are invited to participate in this monitoring process to help determine the standards for learning. Student learning outcomes evidenced by portfolios, student self-assessment, student projects/exhibits, and/or performance events are some examples of alternative methods of assessing the students' attainment of the general education goals.

Five-Year External Evaluation Process. Every five years Bunker Hill hires an outside consultant to conduct a program review. It will do the same for its general education program. In 1997, the Division of Liberal Arts and Sciences will conduct a program review of general education and liberal arts. It will use a responsive evaluation where assessments are keyed directly to the concerns of faculty, students, and administrators with a stake in the results and to the natural methodologies that grow out of the situation at hand rather than follow a predetermined design. This effort will focus at least 70 percent on interviewing faculty, students, and advisory board members, and 30 percent on questionnaires. Guba and Lincoln (1981) describe Stake's responsive model which recommends a heavy reliance on personal interviews with support from questionnaires when the audience is as diversified as the one at Bunker Hill.

The responsive model, featuring personal interviews, maintains as priority the necessity of getting down into the trenches and gaining a real sense of the effectiveness of the evaluation. To rely solely on data received from questionnaires may result in the loss of important information that surfaces only during the interview process. A major challenge facing the team evaluators is to develop the appropriate questions to be used for interviews or questionnaires to elicit meaningful information. The common approach is to base the questions on the anticipated goals of the general education program to be evaluated.

Lessons Learned

First and foremost, a task as comprehensive as the development and implementation of a general education program requires presidential support in terms of funds, resources, faculty, release time, guest speakers and trainers, and administrative cooperation. Second, such a campaign for curriculum change has to be clearly defined, planned, organized, marketed, and endorsed by the college community. Third, communication and feedback systems should be methodically implemented to keep everyone informed about the progress of the general education initiative.

Key to curriculum change on the scale of a general education program at Bunker Hill Community College was the use of a collaborative decision-making model. This model utilized an inclusive approach that invited, considered, and incorporated the participation of faculty, staff, students, trustees, and alumni. This model aimed at providing a safe environment where debate and dissent occurred without any administrative recrimination or punishment. Furthermore, the model relied on negotiation as a method of problem solving and consensual conflict resolution rather than administrative mandate or fiat. The model also acknowledged the important role faculty have in the development and success of any curriculum and the fact that curriculum reform must address academic as well as political concerns. At times, students' learning needs may be overshadowed by divisional and departmental turf and power issues that must be addressed.

The collaborative decision-making model resulted in the implementation of a general education program at Bunker Hill in the fall of 1994. In spring 1991, the general education goals were approved by the College Forum. In spring 1992, the general education model was accepted. The general education implementation process was accepted and approved by the Curriculum Committee in fall 1993 and approved by the College Forum in spring 1994. The college catalogue, degree audit forms, and student academic advising sheets were revised in time for the fall 1994 implementation of the general education program. Last, a brochure was developed that explained the general education goals and model for the students. Admissions, Enrollment Services, Student Advising and Retention Center staff, faculty, academic advisers, and the registrar's office also used this brochure.

In conclusion, a core of common learning enhances the sense of community, whether large or small. Colleges have an obligation to provide students with a plan that specifies the learning that should result from four or more semesters of course preparation. There is an interrelationship that exists among the different disciplines that too often goes unnoticed by graduating students.

They view their college education as simply a piecemeal sequence of course requirements. A general education core can ensure that the student who is transferring to an upper-division college or entering the job market knows these interrelationships exist. Like Boyer and Levine (1981), who argue that an effective college has a clear and vital mission, all members of the Bunker Hill College community have come to understand and promote a shared vision of what the institution is seeking to accomplish with its general education program, namely, the education of well-rounded students who are prepared for the challenges of lifelong learning.

References

Bartkovich, J. *The General Education Component in Vocational Technical Programs Debate: From a Community College Perspective.* Washington, D.C.: American Association of Community and Junior Colleges, July 1981. (ED 208 920)

Boyer, E., and Levine, A. *A Quest for Common Learning.* Washington, D.C.: The Carnegie Foundation for the Advancement of Teaching, 1981.

Gaff, J. G. *General Education Today: A Critical Analysis of Controversies, Practices, and Reforms.* San Francisco: Jossey-Bass, 1983.

Guba, E. and Lincoln, Y. *Effective Evaluation.* San Francisco: Jossey-Bass, 1981.

Levine, A. "Curriculi-Curricula." *Change,* March/April 1990, 22 (2), 46–51.

Lukenbill, J. D., and McCabe, R. H. *General Education in a Changing Society: Miami-Dade Community College.* Dubuque, Iowa: Kendall/Hunt, 1978.

McClenney, K. M. "Principles of Good Practice for Assessing Student Learning." *Leadership Abstracts,* April 1993, 6 (4).

Miller, G. E. *The Meaning of General Education.* New York: Teachers College Press, Columbia University, 1988.

MALINDA M. SMUTEK is dean of liberal arts and sciences at Bunker Hill Community College and successfully managed the General Education Curriculum Reform initiative from its development in 1990 to its implementation in 1994.

*In implementing the general education program at Jefferson
Community College in Louisville, Kentucky, the faculty confronted
the difficulties of ensuring the teaching of competencies across the
curriculum, assessing the effects of general education, and maintaining a balance between integrity to the ideals of general
education and accountability for specific requirements.*

General Education at Jefferson Community College: Accountability and Integrity

Patrick Ecker, Diane Calhoun-French

The faculty and administration of Jefferson Community College in Louisville, Kentucky, have struggled with the shape and implementation of the general education portion of the curriculum for the last several years. The struggle has centered around integrity and accountability: the integrity of what we do and accountability to the state and to the University of Kentucky. We will detail that struggle and suggest what meanings it has for our college. We will begin with a description of the college and its basic structure; then we will enumerate several of the major constraints that have surfaced in considering general education at Jefferson; next we will describe the new general education plan and the problems inherent with its implementation and evaluation; finally, we will suggest some conclusions and directions for the future.

Community Colleges in Kentucky

The structure of public community colleges in the state of Kentucky provides the essential starting point in understanding the complexities of the general education plan at Jefferson. In 1962, the Kentucky General Assembly authorized the University of Kentucky Board of Trustees to establish and operate a system of community colleges across the state. When Jefferson Community College first opened its doors in 1968, it did so as part of the University of Kentucky Community College System. It continues to operate as part of that system today. The general education program in place at Jefferson is the same plan that is in operation at the other thirteen community colleges of the University of Kentucky system. Jefferson participated in the debate over what form the plan should take and assumed responsibility for the specifics of implementation and evaluation.

The University of Kentucky Community College System has always been committed to a strong core of general education in all its instructional programs. Over its history, however, the scope and nature of this component have varied with shifting educational perspectives and changing economic and cultural imperatives. The latest version was developed during the 1992–93 academic year by a committee composed of faculty representatives from each of the fourteen colleges in the University of Kentucky Community College System. Special care was taken to include both general education and technical faculty from a range of academic disciplines. Committee members conveyed ideas, suggestions, and concerns to and from their campus colleagues as the committee did its year-long work. The final recommendations of the committee were forwarded for approval to the UK Community College System Council, also composed of faculty representatives from each college. This body had final authority over curricular matters. However, approval did not occur without considerable objection and debate from the Jefferson representatives and the faculty they represented.

Constraints

When administrators and faculty at the system office in Lexington, and elsewhere across the state, felt the need to revise the general education program to bring it in line with modern standards and trends, community colleges all across the state had to work together to come up with a plan acceptable to the majority. In a sense, this difficult, drawn-out process ultimately benefited everyone because the finished product had input from faculty across the state. At the same time, the major virtue of this system can at times become its major constraint. Satisfying the majority may detract significantly from what an individual college can do to meet its own needs. As the only public community college in Kentucky located in a large metropolitan area, some of Jefferson's concerns are unique. For example, most of our transfer students go to the University of Louisville, others go to Western Kentucky University, Eastern Kentucky University, or to a variety of private four-year institutions. Many students in the eastern part of the state transfer to Morehead State University, while many from the far western part of the state have their sights on Murray State University. Each of these institutions has its own general education program, and somehow the new UK Community College System general education initiative had to complement general education programs in higher education institutions across the state. To suggest, as did the original version of the system general education plan, that technical math would satisfy the mathematics component of general education requirements did not make sense for Jefferson because, for example, the University of Louisville and other four-colleges in our transfer area required college algebra.

A second major constraint centers on the nature of open-door admissions. We admit a large number of students who, for a variety of reasons, are not prepared for college work. This problem is particularly acute in the mathematics area where between 80 and 90 percent of our students need remedial work to acquire the foundation necessary to pass our college algebra class. One of the problems facing the general education initiative in Kentucky in general, and at Jefferson in particular, revolved around the need to have high standards in an open admissions setting. Community colleges across the nation face this challenge.

A third major constraint on the general education curriculum is our commitment to diversity. When the Kentucky community colleges began in the early 1960s, it seemed sufficient in the general education program to enumerate general categories such as American or European history, English literature (and not American literature), and public speaking. With the advent of a more acute awareness of the needs of a diverse student body, it was necessary for the general education committee to take into account more complicated and diverse questions than it had in the past. For example, it no longer made sense to insist on only European or American history; the educated citizen needed to have a larger, global perspective, and general education curricula had to take that into account.

The ever-present problem of fiscal constraint also intruded into the deliberations. The 1990s have brought many changes to the community college theater, but surely none have been as important as increased accountability and decreased levels of funding from the state. The significant decrease in levels of funding for the state-supported schools in Kentucky has resulted in what would have looked strange twenty years ago: significant fundraising efforts. In terms of general education, this has proved to be a potential constraint. For example, while it seemed obvious that some computer literacy component needed to be added to the general education program, it remained problematic where the money would come from to fund such a requirement, particularly at Jefferson where some eleven thousand students were involved.

Faculty and administrators across the state faced many constraints as they struggled with the particulars of how to incorporate changes into the general education curricula and still remain viable in the diverse setting of the state of Kentucky. We have struggled to keep intact the integrity of what we do and believe in while at the same time balancing the need to be accountable to the system and the state of which we are an integral part.

The General Education Curriculum

The present general education program is grounded in the belief that education must "help students become productive people who are aware of the ideas and aspirations which motivate human thought and who can successfully use their understanding of the world, themselves, and their roles in society" (University of Kentucky Community College System, p. 1). Its specific requirements derive from the twelve systemwide competency statements that follow from this. These requirements propose that the graduate of any associate degree program can:

1. Communicate effectively using standard written English
2. Communicate in a clear oral and nonverbal fashion and employ active listening skills
3. Demonstrate basic skills in computer operations and/or software applications
4. Organize, analyze, and make information useful by employing mathematics
5. Demonstrate an awareness of one's interaction with the biological/physical environment
6. Demonstrate an awareness of self as an individual, as a member of a multicultural society, and/or as a member of a world community
7. Recognize the impact of decisive ideas in human heritage
8. Develop and perform basic search strategies and access information in a variety of formats, print and nonprint
9. Analyze, summarize, and interpret a variety of reading materials
10. Think critically and make connections in learning across the disciplines
11. Elaborate upon knowledge to create new thoughts, processes, and products
12. Demonstrate an awareness of ethical considerations in making value choices

These carefully articulated competency statements reflect their developers' overarching philosophy of general education, explicitly presented as background, explanation, and justification in the system document. The writers assert that the curriculum must be of sufficient depth and breadth to meet the needs of all students and that graduates must be "intellectually flexible, articulate, creative, and prepared for continuous growth" (University of Kentucky Community College System, p. 1). This means that students need both an understanding of the contemporary world of work and the specific careers they have chosen and an appreciation for their own talents and interests. Indeed, the general education curriculum must enable students "to develop their own values, to pursue goals, and to contribute to the political, moral, social, and cultural enrichment of society" (p. 1). Students are expected to achieve some of these competencies by enrolling in specific courses; other competencies are to be taught across the curriculum. For each of the first eight competencies, a specific list of courses is given from which students must choose a specified number of hours. For instance, students can choose between two courses enabling them to "communicate effectively using standard written English." There are ninety courses in such disciplines as anthropology, foreign languages, psychology, sociology, and women's studies that students can choose among to ensure that they "demonstrate an awareness of self as an individual, as a member of a multicultural society, and/or as a member of a world community" (p.

3). The last four competencies (9–12) listed above—dealing with reading, integrated learning, creative thinking, and ethics/values—are expected to be taught across the curriculum. In addition, a fifth competency requirement called for writing to be taught across the curriculum as well. Table 4.1 indicates the general education credit-hour requirement for each of the three degrees conferred by Jefferson Community College, as well as the numbers of the twelve competency statements to which they are linked.

This latest version of general education differs from previous curricula in two significant ways. First, there is a common list of courses that satisfies requirements for all degrees, rather than one list for AA and AS programs and another for AAS degrees. This reflects the current and, we believe, healthy blurring of distinctions between "academic" and "technical" programs and the realization that contemporary students need comprehensive skills for the economic marketplace as well as a commitment to lifelong expansion of both their cultural and technical horizons. The new requirements also revise past practice in their inclusion of across-the-curriculum competencies, by far the most controversial aspect of the general education program.

The Challenge of General Education at Jefferson Community College

Although the competencies, course lists, and degree requirements were developed and ratified by the community college system, each individual college was charged with developing its own implementation and evaluation plan. That is, the Jefferson Community College faculty is obligated to specify how it will ensure that across-the-curriculum competencies are being taught and that

Table 4.1. General Education Credit Hour Requirements by Degree

Competency Area	Associate in Arts	Associate in Science	Associate in Applied Science
Writing/Accessing Information (1, 8, 9, 10, 11, 12)	3–6	3–6	3–6
Oral Communication (2, 9, 10, 11, 12)	3	3	3
Computer Literacy (3, 9, 10, 11, 12)	1–3	1–3	1–3
Mathematics (4, 9, 10, 11, 12)	3	4	3
Science (5, 9, 10, 11, 12)	6	12	3
Social Interaction (6, 9, 10, 11, 12)	6	6	3
Heritage/Humanities (7, 9, 10, 11, 12)	6	6	3
Social Interaction or Heritage/Humanities (6, 7, 9, 10, 11, 12)	6		
Total	34–39	35–40	19–24

all general education competencies are indeed being learned. And, while program evaluation is common in Kentucky community colleges, this new emphasis on measuring the outcomes of general education—especially competencies "infused" across the curriculum—reflects a genuinely new climate for education in our state and region.

In an era when accrediting bodies such as the Southern Association of Colleges and Schools emphasize institutional effectiveness, and our legislature's accountability bill ties new funding to specific performance measures, colleges must do a better job of discovering and articulating what our graduates can do. It is no longer sufficient to infer the success of general education curricula and courses from sporadic review of grade distributions, retention data, enrollment and performance in subsequent sequential courses, and transfer performance records. What is necessary is the systematic review of student performance and evidence that this review leads, when appropriate, to substantive change at the course, program, or institutional level. Jefferson Community College is currently wrestling with the form our implementation and evaluation plan should take; our struggles are, we believe, indicative of the problematic accountability and assessment issues that all higher education faces.

Jefferson's Implementation and Evaluation Plan

Before Jefferson faculty began their work on the college's implementation and evaluation plan, some two dozen or so attended a workshop conducted by members of the systemwide General Education Committee. Here they received a copy of the general education guidelines including the competencies, lists of courses acceptable to fulfill course-specific requirements, and the kinds of issues that should be addressed through the across-the-curriculum competencies. They also received an *Implementation Guide* that suggested the kinds of instructional activities that might develop the desired competencies in students. The presenters ended by sharing sample syllabi and assignments from a variety of disciplines. Armed with these materials and background information, the Jefferson faculty were to develop their own plan.

Subsequent to this system-sponsored workshop, Jefferson's academic deans distributed the general education requirements and guidelines to the faculty as a whole. The deans then appointed a collegewide committee composed of representatives from every academic division on each campus to formulate a plan to submit for collegewide faculty approval and forwarding to the UK Community College System. At this writing, such a plan has just been approved and submitted; the system office has not had time to respond or comment.

Discussion of general education implementation has centered around one controversial issue: the teaching of across-the-curriculum competencies. Assessment matters at issue include building consensus around a particular philosophy of evaluation, determining how to appropriately evaluate student attainment of across-the-curriculum competencies, and compiling an array of possible indicators of student success.

Clearly, one way to ensure that the across-the-curriculum competencies are being addressed is to require that every course designated as general education contain experiences that provide for student attainment of every competency. Indeed, a majority of the systemwide General Education Committee advocated precisely this in their workshop, and it appears that a majority of system colleges have adopted this strategy. With this approach, syllabi for each general education course would list the attainment of the five (9–12, plus writing) across-the-curriculum competencies as projected student outcomes. Presumably, the successful course completer would thus have achieved these as well as other course-specific outcomes.

Jefferson Community College's faculty, however, seemed loath to take such a prescriptive approach that required that every competency be addressed in every course. Many felt such a mandate was an infringement on their appropriate roles as determiners of course content. Others expressed concern that, although it would certainly be possible to meet the letter of the general education law with such an approach, its spirit would be better served by acknowledging that certain courses are better vehicles for addressing specific across-the-curriculum competencies than others. Thus, Jefferson's draft document set forth a goal of ensuring that general education competencies would be met in general education courses on an institution-wide basis, using the example that a mathematics instructor would probably spend less time on ethics and values than would a sociology instructor. Following from this, the final approved document further indicates that, although individual syllabi may include statements about across-the-curriculum competencies, such inclusions are not mandatory.

Assessment Issues

Assessment issues in general education have generated an equal amount of discussion at Jefferson, since the decision not to require each syllabus to address the attainment of general education competencies makes their measurement even more problematic. However, this implementation decision is consistent with the assessment philosophy around which the college faculty have developed consensus: evaluation will focus on the institution and its general education program, rather than on individual students. Indeed, such an approach dictates that, although individual student course performance may be indicative of success, holistic measures of achievement that evaluate institutional and program achievement will be more important. Moreover, although multiple indicators of success are needed, such a system permits random sampling of student attainment. And, finally, it obviates the necessity for each general education instructor and course to address student achievement of across-the-curriculum competencies, instead dispersing this responsibility institution wide.

Under its assessment scheme, Jefferson will gather two types of information to ensure that its general education program is successful: information about the extent to which the institution integrates appropriate learning experiences into the curriculum and information about the performance of the students as a whole. The former will require us to ascertain—through survey, review of syllabi and tests, and other methods—that competency-based learning experiences are being provided across the curriculum sufficient to ensure that each student completing the general education curriculum will have the opportunity to achieve each competency. The latter will require us to demonstrate—through multiple quantitative and qualitative indicators—that Jefferson students do indeed attain the competencies to which these learning experiences are directed. Such indicators will include traditional indexes of achievement, like grade distributions, retention data, student evaluation questionnaires, pre- and posttesting, and systemwide employer and student survey instruments. But reliance on such traditional indicators will not be enough—especially in light of the Kentucky Education Reform Act, which is changing the face of elementary and secondary education in our state and promising a new kind of student by the end of the decade. We must also explore the use of focus groups, portfolio evaluation, capstone courses or projects, exit interviews/discussions, and the like to give us the information necessary to serve the student of the twenty-first century.

Lessons Learned

Clearly, there are important lessons to be learned from Jefferson Community College's experiences with the development and implementation of current general education requirements. The first is the importance of broad faculty involvement in the process from the outset. This was certainly recognized by the UK Community College System as it put together a broad and representative systemwide committee. Despite this, however, many faculty members at our institution seemed to believe that their "ownership" of the curriculum was somehow being undermined. It is not enough for faculty to be represented. They must feel—all of them—informed about and involved in a process for which they are ultimately responsible. This will always be difficult for colleges in a system as diverse as Kentucky's.

Our struggle with the implementation of across-the-curriculum competencies also taught us how critically important it is for academic administrators and faculty alike to develop procedures that are flexible, especially when faculty perceive their classroom and instructional prerogatives to be challenged. Many, in fact most, of the Jefferson faculty, whether they are teaching general education or technical courses, address the across-the-curriculum competencies in the classes they teach, in some fashion and to some extent. To insist, however, that their syllabi should explicitly contract them to do so proved almost universally unacceptable to a faculty who take these documents and the obligations they enjoin upon them very seriously.

Finally, this experience has taught us all the importance of keeping focused on our goal: to nurture those qualities in our students that we believe are critical to their future success on the job and in their lives. Our faculty committee could have easily dispatched its task by adopting "legally" correct, but ultimately meaningless, approaches to these new requirements. For instance, every instructor could have technically fulfilled her obligation to teach ethics and values by admonishing the students not to cheat, but opting for the letter of the law rather than its spirit ultimately would have benefited no one, least of all the students. What is important, after all, even in this age of accountability where we must be concerned with the letter of the law, is not ultimately the meeting of curricular prescriptions but the development of students and the integrity of those of us who teach them. Jefferson Community College is committed to access, excellence, and diversity, and we must first and foremost be accountable to these ideals and to ourselves.

Reference

University of Kentucky Community College System, *General Education Requirements,* 1993.

PATRICK ECKER is dean of academic affairs at Jefferson Community College's Downtown Campus in Louisville, Kentucky.

DIANE CALHOUN-FRENCH is dean of academic affairs at Jefferson Community College's Southwest Campus in suburban Louisville, Kentucky.

*A brief review of the collegewide general education program
provides a context for the discussion of specific applications at
the Wolfson Campus that have enriched the scope of the program.*

Miami-Dade Community College: Applications at the Wolfson Campus

Eduardo J. Padrón, Ted Levitt

For many years, events in South Florida have served as precursors to the momentous social, cultural, and economic changes affecting the country. The Cuban revolution in 1959, the Mariel boatlift in 1980, and a constant exodus from impoverished Latin American countries have brought wave after wave of new residents to our shores and changed the personality of South Florida forever. Once famous as a winter vacation spot and retirement home for countless northerners, the region has evolved as one of the most complex, exciting, and turbulent urban areas in the country.

Metropolitan Dade County is now home to more than two million people. According to the 1990 census (U.S. Department of Commerce, 1990), the county is 51 percent Hispanic, with approximately equal numbers of Anglo and African-American populations filling out the mix. Those numbers, however, do not come close to approximating the diversity of culture, thought, and lifestyle that constitute this community. "Hispanic," for example, denotes a multitude of nationalities as well as cultural and social nuances; "African American" implies various regions of this country, Haitian and Jamaican peoples, and a wealth of distinctions in heritage and customs; and the Anglo population can hardly be termed homogeneous, with so many having migrated here from northern climes.

Miami-Dade Community College was founded in 1960 and quickly became the first and often only avenue of personal development for this new Miami multitude. The college's enrollment reflected the massive demographic shifts overtaking and changing the nature of the community. In its inaugural year, the college received 1,338 credit students in temporary quarters; today the college enrolls more than 77,000 credit students and 40,000 noncredit students at five major campuses and numerous outreach centers. Miami-Dade is perhaps *the* prime example in higher education of the new American educational and cultural context; enrollment is more than 57 percent Hispanic, with approximately equal (20 percent) proportions of African-American and Anglo students. Women make up 58 percent of the student body, and the mean age of all students is just over twenty-six (Morris and Folsom, 1994).

The Wolfson Campus profile (Quiroga and Garcia, 1994) further defines this new reality. Located in the heart of downtown Miami, it draws heavily from the city's downtown work force, with more than 50 percent employed in the range of thirty-five hours per week. Commensurately, 65 percent are part-time students, averaging sixteen credits per year. Hispanics make up 68 percent of the credit enrollment, and close to 60 percent speak Spanish or Haitian Creole in their homes. More than half (57 percent) are first generation college students. Each year the Wolfson graduation ceremony opens with a parade of some sixty flags, representing the countries of origin of that year's graduates.

The Challenge of Basic Skills

More than three-quarters of Wolfson's entering students require at least one developmental course, and combined with students in need of English as a Second Language (ESL) course work, fully 84 percent are considered underprepared for college. Approximately half of the student population, based on entry assessment tests, requires developmental assistance in the critical areas of reading and writing.

Traditional approaches to general education assume an adequate proficiency level in the English language and basic academic skills, but clearly, other traditions, both cultural and social, have been at work in this community and the college. At Miami-Dade, we have long recognized that a successful general education format depends, to a large degree, on the attention we are willing to afford basic skills development. Despite strong feelings and varied philosophies within the college community, as well as legislative grumbling and proposals to curtail funding for developmental programs, the college remains steadfast in supporting students' efforts to develop the basic skills necessary to succeed in college and the workplace. In adopting this stance, we are simply responding to an increasingly poignant societal and cultural reality, one that is particularly evident in South Florida. Having said that, it is also important to note that basic skills are not regarded, by any means, as the central aspect of the general education program.

Though not a guiding principle, basic skills development has necessarily drawn the creative energy of both faculty and administrators. In our ESL program, for example, faculty have employed a range of teaching methods to incorporate the general education goal on thinking-skills development into the curriculum. In addition, the college and the Wolfson Campus, via aggressive grantsmanship and faculty ingenuity, have provided students with up-to-theminute technological support and specialized tutoring. And, of course, our developmental courses tie in as an early companion piece for most students in the general education program.

The General Education Program Reforms

In 1974, the college undertook an institutional self-study (Lukenbill and McCabe, 1978) that planted the seeds for the sweeping general education reforms that followed. The study noted a lack of "synthesis and integration within and across courses and disciplines" (p.8) in the then existing general education program. It further assessed the courses as "too often taught as a simplified introduction to a discipline rather than as courses which are part of a program providing a liberal arts foundation" (p.8). In echoing the disappointments of many who have watched general education lose its focus and fall prey to the disciplines, the self-study urged the presentation of a "clear and meaningful rationale for general education courses for faculty and students alike" (p.8).

What followed was a systematic and comprehensive general education study that affected almost every area of the college. The study reasserted the college's mission, addressed a broad spectrum of philosophical and practical issues relative to community colleges and general education, and then proceeded to lay out a new definition and rationale for general education. It also articulated specific goals for the program and generated a new curricular structure and course content.

Definition, Rationale, and Goals. The college's definition of general education reflected not only a respect for the liberal traditions of general education but the emerging understanding of the role of community colleges in American education: general education at Miami-Dade Community College is that aspect of the college's instructional program which has as its fundamental purpose the development and integration of every student's knowledge, skills, attitudes, and experiences so that the student can engage effectively in a life-long process of inquiry and decision making. Most telling, however, in the articulation of the new program was a series of value statements. As the study's authors so aptly put it, "The question 'Why have it?' is directly related to another question, 'What is its worth?' "(Lukenbill and McCabe, 1975, p.5). The highest values were placed on the integration of knowledge drawn from multiple sources leading to effective decision making and practical behavior in daily life. A commitment to the process of self-actualization and a lifetime of learning were joined with an appreciation for the breadth and depth of ideas and the growth of society and its institutions. Clearly, Miami-Dade determined that its program of general education would be, above all, relevant. The edifying value of learning was even superseded by the need to *be a learner,* to actively connect learning to living life in a conscious fashion. Developing the character and the capacities to direct the course of one's own life were practical achievements that higher education could and should foster.

The general education program delineated a set of broad goals that served as guidelines for the curricular development of the program. The goals were divided into six areas: fundamental skills, the individual, the individual's goals for the future, the individual's relationships with other persons and groups, society and the individual, and natural phenomena and the individual. The structure of the program is illustrated in Figure 5.1.

The basic skills courses are required of students whose assessment results indicate a developmental need. All students must complete the five core courses, and AA students are required also to complete the distribution requirement. Students pursuing the Associate in Science degree in one of the occupational or allied health programs, or the Associate in General Studies, are only required to complete the core. They are afforded a broader range of course choices in order to clarify their career plans.

The Core Courses and Distribution Groups. The five core courses sit at the heart of the general education program, representing areas of personal and academic development. These courses were not designed merely to introduce the disciplines; rather, the primary aim of the core courses was, and remains, to assist students in achieving the goals of the general education program. The core courses are taken early in a student's program and provide necessary and valuable input even for those students who do not complete degrees or "stop out" for a period of time. However, students are not required to complete the core prior to taking other courses, and, in fact, they are encouraged to mix distribution group courses with core courses.

To complete the twenty-one credit distribution group requirement, students must take at least one course from each distribution group, including the one required course at the distribution level, English composition. They can opt out of a second distribution requirement in composition by achieving good performance in the core and first distribution composition courses. The courses in the distribution groups were designed to further fulfill the goals of the general education program and introduce students to the principles and basic methods in these areas. The number of courses in the distribution groups is relatively small, directing students to courses that are more general in approach.

Figure 5.1. General Education Requirements for an Associate in Arts

Basic Skills	
Math Competency (Required for Graduation)	Reading and Writing Competency (Required for Core Communications Course)

General Education Core — 15 Credits				
Communications	Humanities	Social Environment	Natural Environment	Individual

Distribution Groups — 21 Credits				
Communications	Humanities	Social Sciences	Natural Sciences	Physical Education

Program Assessment and the CLAST. For the past decade, Florida's community college students, as well as all state university students completing their second year, have been required to take the College Level Academic Skills Test (CLAST). The exam has been a source of controversy and frustration statewide. Many educators, at Miami-Dade and throughout the state, have long considered the test a gatekeeper with particularly adverse effects on minority students. The competencies have been seriously questioned, and it is widely believed that the test fails as a gauge of the effectiveness of the general education program. In fact, the primary criticisms center on the additional course work required to prepare for the CLAST competencies and the richness of advanced course offerings that is lost. At present, a statewide committee is reviewing the CLAST and its effect on students.

The Wolfson Campus

The general education study and subsequent implementation brought a unified philosophy and structure to general education collegewide. Each of Miami-Dade's five campuses, however, was encouraged to address the needs of its particular student body, highlighting content and developing pedagogy that would fulfill the general education goals. At the Wolfson Campus, a number of principal themes have emerged, some already articulated in the general education rationale and others particular to our constituency and expertise. Specific applications—course modules—regarding environmental awareness, interactive technology, multicultural awareness and global thinking, individualized and interdisciplinary learning, and thinking-skills development have all contributed to the unique character of the general education program at the Wolfson Campus.

EDGE: Environmental Dimensions in General Education. The Wolfson Campus Environmental Center and Environmental Ethics Institute have combined, since 1976, to offer a wide range of credit and noncredit courses to South Floridians. In 1990, faculty from the institute took up the investigation of "earth literacy," a term coined by the historic Club of Rome in *No Limits to Learning* (Botkin, 1979). In this volume, the authors sought to broaden the scope of knowledge to include "earth literacy," a deeper understanding of the planet and our relationship to it.

Environmental Dimensions for General Education (EDGE) was born from this appreciation of the need for earth literacy. EDGE seeks to integrate within the general education program an appreciation of the human-earth relationship. By generating in students an awareness of that relationship and a practical concern for environmental issues, we also are providing an important context for critical thinking and intelligent decision making, important values of the general education program.

EDGE began with seven faculty members from throughout the curriculum meeting for lunch on a weekly basis for one semester with faculty from the Environmental Ethics Institute. Once they gained a working understanding of earth literacy, the faculty in attendance began developing resources suitable to their disciplines. The aim was to create modules that would fit seamlessly into existing core and distribution courses, providing context for the general education goals, as well as introducing an enriched environmental awareness.

Communications. A two-part teaching module for the English composition core course offered fifteen literary selections—poems, essays, and a short story, as well as selected audiotapes—all exemplary for their literary quality and the challenging environmental issues they articulate. Describing the works as stimulating "self-reflective" and "earth-reflective" thought, the module's creator included author biographies and discussion and essay questions. The second section, intended for any American literature course, presents four supplemental bibliographies of American literature as seen through an environmental/earth literate perspective. The bibliography chronicles an American literary tradition concerned with the relationship of men and women to the land. The names of Thoreau, Hawthorne, Melville, Whitman, Twain, and later Faulkner, Hemingway, Frost, and Steinbeck ensure a literate and thoughtful elevation of our environmental concerns.

The Social Environment. Students in this core course benefited from the efforts of a member of our social science faculty who is regarded as one of Florida's premier historians. He designed a guided walking tour of downtown Miami, highlighting the environmental paradise that was Miami as recently as 100 years ago and the degradation of this environment that accompanied the city's development. Via supplemental readings, a wealth of historical and environmental data, pretour exercises, and a posttour follow-up, students are encouraged to assess their personal "sense of place," exploring the notions of neighborhood, community, tradition, and home in the context of the physical region they inhabit. This module has also been effectively used in U.S., Florida, and Miami history courses.

Humanities. The title of the humanities module, "A Re-enchantment with the Natural World Through Art," (Gottlieb-Roberts, 1990) has pointed our students toward an invaluable reordering of perspective, on both the environment and their own perceptual capacity. Utilizing progressive public art as an evocative setting, the module strikes at our "adult" tendency to separate or detach from the phenomena that surround us. By reinvesting in their own direct experience, through art, students are addressing an attitude that is, as the module's creator states, "tragically manifest in our abuse of the environment" (p. 2). Utilizing preparatory materials, lecture and slides, and a tour of an example of public art, this module assists students to connect their sensory experience to what they feel and to develop and trust their intuition, all essential qualities in valuing the environment.

Equally creative and effective modules have been created for the social science and natural environment core courses, a mathematics distribution group offering, and for English as a Second Language.

Applying Multimedia in General Education Curriculum. For the past three years members of the Wolfson Campus faculty have invested untold hours in the development of multimedia applications for the classroom. With the help of grants from the National Endowment for the Humanities and utilizing the emergent CD-ROM technology, they have combined text, audio, slides, and video segments into the production of nineteen laser discs for use throughout the curriculum. These interactive modules include an examination of four major ethnic groups in Miami via their religion, music, and history; the presentation of various works of art with a range of critical statements, challenging students' thinking and writing skills; a visit to the theaters of Greece, Rome, England, France, and the United States, exploring historical examples and modern playwrights; and an exposition of certain philosophical and ethical approaches to the study of our natural environment.

These topics and a host of others are brought to multimedia life, providing a teaching tool that we could not have imagined when the original general education reforms were instituted. Through multimedia creations, we are addressing an ever more dominant, visual learning style in our students. We live in a culture rapidly transforming itself from a spoken and written tradition to one that is image based and image conscious. The following example of classroom-based multimedia has provided successful learning experiences for students who are often unaccustomed or uncomfortable with the traditional academic culture that appeals to a more auditory/conceptual learning style.

Social Science and Humanities Case Study: ECOVERDE. The mythical nation of ECOVERDE provides the context for an extraordinary interdisciplinary, critical-thinking and decision-making exercise. Students are presented with striking topographical, social, and cultural graphics combined with a data base of existing natural resources, demographics, ethnic composition, historical background, and political conditions. Students develop the country's economic, social, and political life, choosing from among numerous options and dealing with the ramifications of their decisions. The exercise, which can be spread over numerous class meetings, allows for both individual and group skills development. The module encourages thinking-skills competency as well as several of the specific conceptual and content requirements from the various core courses. ECOVERDE has been used in the humanities and social and natural environment core courses, as well as in additional elective offerings.

Multicultural Awareness and Global Thinking. We cannot help but be aware of the variation in culture and ethnicity that has converged on the Wolfson Campus. The campus and the community exist as a natural laboratory for exploring the impact of diverse, culturally rooted understandings on the canon of the general education curriculum. We needed, however, to supplement our natural atmosphere with a structure that would ensure that cultural perspectives were aired and allowed to influence the discussion. Again, we have adopted a modular/infusion approach, designed to integrate with the established course content.

The goals of internationalizing the curriculum have a familiar ring: to provide students with a competitive advantage in the economic marketplace by acquiring foreign language skills, geographic knowledge, and cultural understanding; to demonstrate the diversity of the world's cultures, their comparative development and transformation; and to transcend ethnocentric attitudes—to see beyond the "I and mine" mentality to the importance of communicating effectively with others.

Folktales and Their Role in the Development of Cultures and Individuals. This generic module has proved applicable in no fewer than four of the core courses. The module explores various versions of a single folktale in cultures around the world. Students are introduced to the fable's archetypes and adult themes and asked to explore their own experience. Not only are they able to appreciate the universality of certain elements, but they can also discover new understandings particular only to other cultures and times. Language and literature also take on a new dimension, displaying the power to communicate the beliefs and dreams of a nation's people.

The Individual in Transition. This module, for the psychology core course of the same name, asks students to articulate their personal experience relative to particular psychological phenomena. Alternate perceptions of consciousness, healing, personality formation, and psychopathology, as well as a reassessment of major schools of psychological thought are considered in the context of the students' multinational experience. The effect is to display the universal nature of the most basic of emotional and psychological experiences and to underscore cultural impact on these phenomena. Each person's approach to his or her life, to problem-solving strategies, as well as to notions of "normal" and "abnormal" are seen in a new light. Using the established knowledge base and addressing the course competencies, the module offers the students a new dimension of experience, broadening the impact of the general education curriculum.

Additional modules have been developed for the core courses in communications, addressing competencies in mechanical and grammatical skills and library research. These modules use readings and written work pertaining to the theme of the global village and the social environment, as well as systematic analysis of a foreign culture to develop competencies in communications. Modules have also been developed for several of the distribution courses.

Life Lab and Open College: Cultivating Individual Responsibility. In America's new educational reality, the myth of the eighteen-year-old enrolled at State U., graduating four years later, and moving on to professional life or graduate study has quietly been dispelled. Behind the public perception are six million adults enrolled in community college credit courses, two-thirds of them attending on a part-time basis, and all seeking degrees and certificates. Their average age is twenty-nine, and their educational lives reflect the complexity of their adult years and the times in which they live. They "stop out" for a range of compelling reasons and return to school renewed, not once, but often two and three times before they achieve their degrees. Life Lab and Open College are Wolfson's attempt to provide academic offerings for students willing to apply their maturity to an independent studies program. In both programs, on-campus class time is exchanged for mentor-student advisories, independent research, and relevant practicum activities.

Life Lab offers four of the five core courses and five additional distribution-level courses, as well as some fifty elective offerings in an altered format. The core course in English composition is a prerequisite to ensure the necessary reading and writing skills. With diminished class time, both Life Lab and Open College require a great deal more written product to confirm mastery of the subject matter and competencies. In fact, Life Lab is primarily a competency- and contract-based program. The student contracts for a particular grade—A, B, or C—and then designs and completes a study plan to meet the agreed upon requirements. Included in the plan are projected writings (a minimum of three thousand written words per course) and practicum or volunteer involvement. Students are also required to attend a weekly peer group meeting with a faculty facilitator to share and discuss their progress.

Open College also relies on the adviser-student relationship with little formal class time. The program is less practicum oriented, relying more heavily on student writing to confirm understanding of the course competencies. The ability to think systematically, critically, and creatively in identifying problems, analyzing alternate solutions, and making decisions, as indicated in the general education goals, is plumbed through competency-related discussion questions and essay examinations at regular intervals.

Thinking-Skills Development. In addition to basic skills deficiencies, many of our students arrive with a conspicuous lack of development in the realm of thinking skills. Poor reading and writing skills have undeniably affected thinking habits, and the complex of deficiencies presents a major teaching and learning challenge. Regardless, the mandate of the general education program is clear; we have proceeded to teach thinking even as basic skills are being mastered.

In fact many of the tools and methods developed by our faculty for the general education core and distribution offerings have been directly applicable in ESL courses and basic skills. Most are geared to particular disciplines and subjects, while others are more generic and apply throughout the curriculum. In addition, in each of the past four years, the Wolfson Campus, now in partnership with Dade County Public Schools, has sponsored the National Conference on Instructional Applications of Critical Thinking, showcasing not only our own faculty's efforts but the work of seventy to eighty teachers from across the country.

Through our own Teaching and Learning Resource Center we have circulated the models developed by faculty members to their colleagues throughout the campus and college. We have seen the introduction of thinking-skills methods in every core course and many of the distribution courses. Our faculty have developed teaching tools utilizing drama, poetry, and storytelling; developed methods that specifically tie together writing and thinking; assisted students with the development of memory and note-taking strategies; taught improved thinking and decision making in the context of developmental mathematics; developed interactive, multimedia programs of their own, and much more. These faculty members have seen our students' developmental predicament not as an impediment but as fertile ground for teaching thinking skills.

To emphasize thinking-skills competency throughout the curriculum requires an environment that fosters such skills on an everyday basis, not only in the classroom but throughout the institution. The new Wolfson Campus Thinking Skills Institute will provide a forum for development efforts in methods, interdisciplinary programs, and assessment. The nucleus of faculty who have been able to formalize and share the tools and methods that they use in the classroom serve as leaders in developing a campuswide ethic on critical thinking.

Final Thoughts

Both the mission of the community college and the goals of general education remain quite simple. In a phrase it might read, "Educate all the people who are willing with all the knowledge and skills required for a lifetime of learning." Obviously, simple does not imply easy. In spite of the promise of the programs described here, we know there are major challenges that remain unfulfilled. Alas, for all of the intelligence and wisdom embodied in our institutions, higher education is not a patient realm; yet that is the essential requirement of this endeavor. The fundamental traditions of liberal arts education remain valid, yet they are continually being stretched and challenged by a culture and society that is diversifying and redefining itself in exponential leaps.

The truth is that all the profound changes in the universe will not significantly alter the nature of human learning, and it is to that nature that our learning institutions must bear allegiance. Indeed, we will continue to teach our students to read and write and add numbers *and* to appreciate the full range of human enterprise. Vision, intelligence, and creativity will be required on our part, not to mention a good deal of patience.

References

Botkin, J. W. *No Limits to Learning.* New York: Elsevier Science, 1979.

Gottlieb-Roberts, M. "A Re-enchantment with the Natural World Through Art." In T. McGuirl and N. Watkins (eds.), *EDGE: Environmental Dimension in General Education.* Miami, Fla.: Miami-Dade Community College, Wolfson Campus, Environmental Ethics Institute, 1990.

Lukenbill, J. D., and McCabe, R. H. *General Education in a Changing Society.* Dubuque, Iowa: Kendall/Hunt, 1978.

Morris, K., and Folsom, S. *Fall Student Profile: 1993–94 Closing Fall Enrollment Analysis.* Department of Institutional Research, Miami-Dade Community College, 1994.

Quiroga, M., and Garcia, R. *Composite Profile of the Wolfson Campus Student.* Departments of Testing and Campus Retention, Miami-Dade Community College, Wolfson Campus, 1994.

U.S. Department of Commerce, Census Bureau. *1990 U.S. Census Report.* Washington, D.C.: Government Printing Office, 1990.

EDUARDO J. PADRÓN *is president of Miami-Dade Community College.*

TED LEVITT *is coordinator of Special Academic Projects at the Wolfson Campus, Miami-Dade Community College.*

General education reform in Minnesota's community colleges
began with a statewide agenda for improving student transfer.

The Minnesota Model for General Education

Nancy Register Wangen

General education reform in Minnesota's community colleges is a "story within a story." At its center, the story is about faculty redesign of general education at each of the twenty-one campuses across the state. But general education reform began with a collaboration extending across the four higher education systems, involving community college faculty and their colleagues from seven state universities, four campuses of the University of Minnesota, and thirty-five technical college campuses. Getting a sense of the whole story is important to understanding how and why statewide reform is becoming a reality. This chapter will provide: (1) a brief introduction to the colleges that make up Minnesota's statewide Community College System, (2) an overview of the forces behind reform and the collaborative agenda that defined it, (3) an introduction to the Minnesota Transfer Curriculum (MNTC), (4) a review of the MNTC implementation at the community colleges, and (5) an assessment of the challenges remaining.

The Community Colleges of Minnesota

It has been said that community colleges are a good place to start, no matter how far you want to go. Potential students reading the opening sentence in the system's "viewbook" would find supporting evidence in an experienced faculty, a network of good transfer relationships, state support that covers about two-thirds of tuition costs, and geographic accessibility. No matter where one lives in Minnesota—the northern woods, the southern plains, the lake country, or the growing metropolitan area around Minneapolis and St. Paul—there is a community college nearby. Most are, by national standards, relatively small institutions.

The stated mission of Minnesota's community colleges is comprehensive, but because the state also supports a network of two-year technical colleges, the community colleges are, in practice, somewhat more liberal arts and transfer oriented than comparable colleges in some other states. That will change with a three-way merger of higher education systems in 1995. A number of community colleges and technical colleges located in the same communities are already planning to become single institutions. Most already have a base of shared Associate in Applied Science (AAS) programs where community colleges provide the liberal arts or general education courses and the technical colleges the occupational courses. Beginning in 1995, liberal arts courses in all AAS programs will be selected from the Minnesota Transfer Curriculum described later in this chapter.

For now, the nineteen colleges and two college centers form a statewide system with a central office in St. Paul that provides fiscal, computer, and personnel services to all. The chancellor's staff provides leadership and coordination in academic affairs, student services, faculty development, legislative relations, facilities planning, and research. It is a system in which many relationships cross college boundaries. Faculty and administrators meet separately and together in faculty-led (and administrator-supported) initiatives, including writing across the curriculum, computing across the curriculum, or projects on critical thinking and classroom research that are all part of the systemwide Center of Teaching and Learning. Task forces and work groups address assessment of student learning in developmental education, write policies on student progress, and, more recently, support reform of general education.

In summary, there is a receptivity within the community college system to collaboration that addresses issues of teaching and learning, as well as an expectation of working across college boundaries to address common problems. Very early in our general education reform efforts it became clear that all of these ongoing activities built the critical base of faculty support and leadership that is so essential to reform.

The Forces Behind Reform: Agenda

Everyone working in education knows that good ideas for reform are everywhere, yet few of these good ideas are ever developed sufficiently to become part of the institution. Why is it that a project as large as the Minnesota Transfer Curriculum has come this far and is still moving forward? A short list of elements that made a difference in getting started would have to include leadership, assigned responsibility, clear goals to be achieved, and timing.

Leadership. By 1990, budgets for higher education were not keeping pace with enrollment growth. Chief academic officers in Minnesota's four public college and university systems wanted to know how other institutions were coping with growing numbers of students and proportionately fewer dollars. A joint meeting in August of 1990 produced a long list of shared concerns, including two priorities: student transfer and the quality and coherence of general or liberal education. Briefly, chief academic officers felt that Minnesota needed to move beyond the "nuts and bolts" approach to student transfer reflected in agreements of the 1980s. They saw growing numbers of students taking general education courses from two or more institutions, each with its own notion of what general education should be. Students who were merely meeting distribution requirements most likely viewed their general education courses as separate, unrelated experiences. The "chiefs" recognized that faculty were the key to improving student mobility and to reforming general or liberal education. Faculty collaboration on these two issues, they believed, would help to build trust and mutual respect among institutions that were educating many of the same students.

Assigned responsibility. If faculty collaboration was to be successful, someone needed to set and keep to an agenda, preferably someone perceived as a neutral party. Responsibility for managing the process of collaboration was assigned to an office of Intersystem Collaboration. Its work included shepherding faculty development of the Minnesota Transfer Curriculum, writing its competencies and redrafts, staffing the articulation councils, managing a statewide transfer logistics committee and a network of transfer specialists, running workshops, writing a newsletter and documents, and serving as staff to the chief academic officers.

Clear goals. Student transfer worked as the mechanism for addressing other issues, providing external pressure for good changes. The collaboration agenda had goals that were narrowly focused and realizable. Two indispensable principles formed the foundation of this approach: (1) colleges and universities would accept responsibility for making transfer of credit simpler and more predictable, and (2) all students, transfer and nontransfer alike, would receive comparable treatment. The transfer agenda had four parts:

1. *The Minnesota Transfer Standards* would define clear transfer pathways and common procedures for transfer at all campuses.
2. *Articulation Councils* would build an ongoing faculty communication structure to focus on curriculum and build trust among faculty.
3. *Data* would be more systematically collected to develop a full picture of student mobility and performance.
4. *The Minnesota Transfer Curriculum,* a competency-based approach to general education, would be the centerpiece, the major effort.

Timing. Some good ideas fail because they do not match institutional concerns of the moment. Transfer became a "hot" issue in 1991 when the state legislature issued a mandate to all systems to solve specific transfer problems. The second priority, reform of general education, already had some support from public colleges and universities. A committee had begun work on a new liberal education program at the University of Minnesota, Twin Cities Campus.

Several state universities and community colleges were working on their general education programs or writing student competencies. These internal efforts would be supported by the pressure of an external agenda. The stage was set for timely reform.

The Minnesota Transfer Curriculum

Minnesota's version of a redesigned general education curriculum began by defining the Minnesota Transfer Curriculum.

Principles and Design. By fall of 1995, each community college in Minnesota will offer its version of a redesigned general education curriculum, four years after the first summer workshop when faculty from public colleges and universities met to begin definition of the Minnesota Transfer Curriculum. Two conditions had been agreed to by chief academic officers before that first workshop: (1) the general education curriculum would be competency based, that is, it would identify the student learning to be expected from general or liberal education, and (2) faculty in collaboration across systems would define the common goals and competencies to be achieved, while reserving the actual design of curriculum—the means to achieve the competencies—to faculty at each campus. Faculty at the first of several workshops developed guidelines of their own, including:

1. The expectation of equivalent learning in comparable courses or programs at all institutions
2. Faculty certification of its students' satisfactory completion of its transfer curriculum
3. Completion of an institution's transfer curriculum (or an Associate in Arts degree) to satisfy the lower-division general education requirements at any public university

The first transfer curriculum, distributed to all campuses in the fall of 1991, consisted of an introduction, guidelines, and ten areas of emphasis, each with a general statement of goals. Student competencies were written later by faculty groups meeting in each of the ten areas of emphasis to add some flesh to the bones of a general education curriculum.

In 1992, nearly two hundred faculty representing four systems and more than fifty colleges and universities met for two days to review and critique the draft of the Minnesota Transfer Curriculum. The many pages of comments and discussion summaries were subsequently forwarded to a redraft committee. Faculty, supporting the notion of a competency-based curriculum, asked that no particular distribution of credits be specified. A sixty quarter credit minimum would be the sole reference to credits. Two redrafts later—in January of 1993 and 1994—a final version incorporating most of the recommendations of faculty from all four systems was accepted by the chief academic officers for implementation on all campuses.

   Rationale. The Minnesota Transfer Curriculum is a response to the question, "What should a liberally educated person in our time know and be able to do?" It recognizes that although competence in writing, in critical thinking, and in modes of inquiry are essential, the educated person also needs content and an awareness of values to think clearly about and solve problems. This particular view of general education stretches but does not sever ties with tradition. It maintains traditional discipline areas, such as the natural sciences or the humanities and fine arts, while adding an emphasis on process that engages students in the structure and ways of thinking unique to each discipline.

   Competencies encourage students to use the methods of a discipline and to become participants in learning. Beyond the knowledge and skill areas, four themes—human diversity, global perspective, ethical and civic responsibility, and people and the environment—bring world issues to the classroom, helping students understand that problem solving in today's world is an interdisciplinary challenge. Competencies in the four theme areas require students to apply their knowledge as well as to examine their own beliefs. Faculty are challenged to embed critical thinking in courses across the curriculum.

   All competencies will be achieved at an academic level appropriate to lower-division general education. The ten areas of emphasis are summarized in Table 6.1. In addition to these competencies, students will be expected to use computers, libraries, and other appropriate technology and information resources. Institutions should assure integration of these skills in courses throughout the general education curriculum.

Curricular and Instructional Formats

Once the systemwide goals and competencies were specified, each campus was allowed to develop its own curriculum design for meeting them. The options for curriculum design are as far-reaching as faculty imagination, but to focus discussion on community college campuses, a small faculty group designed three different curricular models that illustrated the range of possibilities. First is the Traditional Model with separate, discrete courses that address competencies in one, or at most two, of the ten goal areas. This model would most likely offer a course in "critical thinking" or a course on "human diversity" rather than embedding the competencies in, for example, sociology or literature courses. Colleges using this model would most likely specify a credit distribution.

   The second, called the Nontraditional Model, would cluster courses around common themes and issues or pair them, perhaps linking an intellectual skills course with a content course. Students might register concurrently for a biology and political science course jointly addressing "Ethics and the Environment." The advantages of a learning community could be realized through faculty collaboration and the time students and faculty would spend together.

   The third curricular model for general education was dubbed the Utopian, because the proposed changes in structure and in interdisciplinary teaching

Table 6.1. The MNTC Goals and Competencies

1. Communication	**Goal:** To develop writers and speakers who use the English language effectively and who read, write, speak, and listen critically. As a base, all students should complete introductory communication requirements early in their collegiate studies. Writing competency is an ongoing process to be reinforced through writing-intensive courses and writing across the curriculum. Speaking and listening skills need reinforcement through multiple opportunities for interpersonal communication, public speaking, and discussion.
Student Competencies	Students will be able to: A. Understand/demonstrate the writing and speaking processes through invention, organization, drafting, revision, editing, and presentation B. Participate effectively in groups with emphasis on listening, critical and reflective thinking, and responding C. Locate, evaluate, and synthesize in a responsible manner material from diverse sources and points of view D. Select appropriate communication choices for specific audiences E. Construct logical and coherent arguments F. Use authority, point-of-view, and individual voice and style in their writing and speaking G. Employ syntax and usage appropriate to academic disciplines and the professional world
2. Critical Thinking	**Goal:** To develop thinkers who are able to unify factual, creative, rational, and value-sensitive modes of thought. Critical thinking will be taught and used throughout the general education curriculum in order to develop students' awareness of their own thinking and problem-solving procedures. To integrate new skills into their customary ways of thinking, students must be actively engaged in practicing thinking skills and applying them to open-ended problems.
Student Competencies	Students will be able to: A. Gather factual information and apply it to a given problem in a manner that is relevant, clear, comprehensive, and conscious of possible bias in the information selected B. Imagine and seek out a variety of possible goals, assumptions, interpretations, or perspectives which can give alternative meanings or solutions to given situations or problems C. Analyze the logical connections among the facts, goals, and implicit assumptions relevant to a problem or claim; generate and evaluate implications that follow from them D. Recognize and articulate the value assumptions which underlie and affect decisions, interpretations, analyses, and evaluations made by ourselves and others

3. Natural Sciences

Goal: To improve students' understanding of natural science principles and of the methods of scientific inquiry, i.e., the ways in which scientists investigate natural science phenomena. As a basis for lifelong learning, students need to know the vocabulary of science and to realize that while a set of principles has been developed through the work of previous scientists, ongoing scientific inquiry and new knowledge will bring changes in some of the ways scientists view the world. By studying the problems that engage today's scientists, students learn to appreciate the importance of science in their lives and to understand the value of scientific perspective. Students should be encouraged to study both the biological and physical sciences.

Student Competencies

Students will be able to:

A. Demonstrate understanding of scientific theories
B. Formulate and test hypotheses by performing laboratory, simulation, or field experiments in at least two of the natural science disciplines. One of these experimental components should develop, in greater depth, students' laboratory experience in the collection of data, its statistical and graphical analysis, and an appreciation of its sources of error and uncertainty
C. Communicate their experimental findings, analyses, and interpretations both orally and in writing
D. Evaluate societal issues from a natural science perspective, ask questions about the evidence presented, and make informed judgments about science-related topics and policies

4. Mathematical/Logical Reasoning

Goal: To increase students' knowledge about mathematical and logical modes of thinking. This will enable students to appreciate the breadth of applications of mathematics, evaluate arguments, and detect fallacious reasoning. Students will learn to apply mathematics, logic, and/or statistics to help them make decisions in their lives and careers. Minnesota's public higher education systems have agreed that developmental mathematics includes the first three years of a high school mathematics sequence through intermediate algebra. (Recommendation from the intersystem Mathematics Articulation Council. Adopted by all systems in February 1992.)

Student Competencies

Students will be able to:

A. Illustrate historical and contemporary applications of mathematical/logical systems
B. Clearly express mathematical/logical ideas in writing
C. Explain what constitutes a valid mathematical/logical argument (proof)
D. Apply higher-order problem-solving and/or modeling strategies

Table 6.1. The MNTC Goals and Competencies *(continued)*

5. History and the Social and Behavioral Sciences	*Goal:* To increase students' knowledge of how historians and social and behavioral scientists discover, describe, and explain the behaviors and interactions among individuals, groups, institutions, events, and ideas. Such knowledge will better equip students to understand themselves and the roles they play in addressing the issues facing humanity.
Student Competencies	Students will be able to: A. Employ the methods and data that historians and social and behavioral scientists use to investigate the human condition B. Examine social institutions and processes across a range of historical periods and cultures C. Use and critique alternative explanatory systems or theories D. Develop and communicate alternative explanations or solutions for contemporary social issues
6. The Humanities and Fine Arts	*Goal:* To expand students' knowledge of the human condition and human cultures, especially in relation to behavior, ideas, and values expressed in works of human imagination and thought. Through study in disciplines such as literature, philosophy, and the fine arts, students will engage in critical analysis, form aesthetic judgments, and develop an appreciation of the arts and humanities as fundamental to the health and survival of any society. Students should have experiences in both the arts and humanities.
Student Competencies	Students will be able to: A. Demonstrate awareness of the scope and variety of works in the arts and humanities B. Understand those works as expressions of individual and human values within an historical and social context C. Respond critically to works in the arts and humanities D. Engage in the creative process or interpretive performance E. Articulate an informed personal reaction to works in the arts and humanities
7. Human Diversity	*Goal:* To increase students' understanding of individual and group differences (e.g., race, gender, class) and their knowledge of the traditions and values of various groups in the United States. Students should be able to evaluate the United States' historical and contemporary responses to group differences.
Student Competencies	Students will be able to: A. Understand the development of and the changing meanings of group identities in the United States' history and culture

B. Demonstrate an awareness of the individual and institutional dynamics of unequal power relations between groups in contemporary society

C. Analyze their own attitudes, behaviors, concepts, and beliefs regarding diversity, racism, and bigotry

D. Describe and discuss the experience and contributions (political, social, economic, etc.) of the many groups that shape American society and culture, in particular those groups that have suffered discrimination and exclusion

E. Demonstrate communication skills necessary for living and working effectively in a society with great population diversity

8. Global Perspective

Goal: To increase students' understanding of the growing interdependence of nations and peoples and develop their ability to apply a comparative perspective to crosscultural social, economic, and political experiences.

Student Competencies

Students will be able to:

A. Describe and analyze political, economic, and cultural elements which influence relations of states and societies in their historical and contemporary dimensions

B. Demonstrate knowledge of cultural, social, religious, and linguistic differences

C. Analyze specific international problems, illustrating the cultural, economic, and political differences that affect their solution

D. Understand the role of a world citizen and the responsibility world citizens share for the common global future

9. Ethical and Civic Responsibility

Goal: To develop students' capacity to identify, discuss, and reflect upon the ethical dimensions of political, social, and personal life and to understand the ways in which they can exercise responsible and productive citizenship. While there are diverse views of social justice or the common good in a pluralistic society, students should learn that responsible citizenship requires them to develop skills to understand their own and others' positions, be part of the free exchange of ideas, and function as public-minded citizens.

Student Competencies

Students will be able to:

A. Examine, articulate, and apply their own ethical views

B. Understand and apply core concepts (for example, politics, rights and obligations, justice, liberty) to specific issues

C. Analyze and reflect on the ethical dimensions of legal, social, and scientific issues

D. Recognize the diversity of political motivations and interests of others

E. Identify ways to exercise the rights and responsibilities of citizenship

Table 6.1. The MNTC Goals and Competencies (*continued*)

10. People and the Environment	*Goal:* To improve students' understanding of today's complex environmental challenges. Students will examine the interrelatedness of human society and the natural environment. Knowledge of both bio-physical principles and socio-cultural systems is the foundation for integrative and critical thinking about environmental issues.
Student Competencies	Students will be able to: A. Explain the basic structure and function of various natural ecosystems and of human adaptive strategies within those systems B. Discern patterns and interrelationships of bio-physical and socio-cultural systems C. Describe the basic institutional arrangements (social, legal, political, economic, religious) that are evolving to deal with environmental and natural resource challenges D. Evaluate critically environmental and natural resource issues in light of understandings about inter-relationships, ecosystems, and institutions E. Propose and assess alternative solutions to environmental problems F. Articulate and defend the actions they would take on various environmental issues

are the most far-reaching. This model would embed intellectual skills and themes into each of four traditional knowledge areas in a two- or three-quarter course. For example, critical thinking, communication, and the four themes of the transfer curriculum would be addressed as appropriate in extended courses in the four traditional discipline groupings of natural sciences, history and the behavioral sciences, the fine arts and humanities, and mathematics/logical systems.

Planning for Implementation

Faculty interest in teaching and learning, nourished by a history of collaboration across college lines, has made systemwide general education reform possible. Both faculty leaders and administrators have rallied to support changes.

Faculty Support. Faculty leaders involved at the outset have stayed involved. The president of the statewide Minnesota Community College Faculty Association has been an effective advocate for innovation in teaching, attention to student learning, and, now, for the reform of general education. Another strong voice has been that of a faculty member present at the first discussion of a transfer curriculum. He summed up the feeling of others, too, when he said, "If this were just about transfer, my interest would have waned; but it's really about general education reform, and that energizes me." He and the vice chancellor visited all campuses for dialogues with faculty about general education and the transfer curriculum. He also chairs the systemwide Task Force on General Education and continues to provide counsel to campus committees working on implementation. Other "faculty champions" are effectively working on their college curriculum committees, on articulation councils, or as leaders in their departments.

Budget for Implementation. A budget request assembled by a small working committee of faculty, academic administrators, and project leaders from the Center for Teaching and Learning was approved by college presidents and by the governing board. New activities to be funded included support for campus efforts to reform general education. In the year before the fall 1995 implementation, the following activities were planned: (1) A small faculty resource team in each of the curriculum areas will provide leadership to showcase "best general education practices," to develop models of outcomes for student learning and/or assessment strategies, and to plan workshops for faculty. (2) One statewide conference with teams from all campuses will look at options for curriculum design. (3) Small grants will be awarded to faculty to carry out innovative general education projects such as pilots of interdisciplinary teaching or paired courses. (4) Special workshops will address at least two of the four theme areas. All faculty development leaders are networking to be certain that all activities provide more opportunities for general education reform. At the campus level, two representative colleges illustrate the structural and substantive issues of implementation.

General Education Reform in a Large College. Reform began at this college in the Minneapolis-St. Paul metropolitan area in spring of 1993 with a multimedia presentation for all by a core of faculty involved in development of the transfer curriculum. In the presentation, faculty and administrators being interviewed about the MNTC were asked difficult questions about academic freedom and college autonomy. After viewing the presentation, faculty divided into discipline groups for discussions focused on issues they identified.

On this campus, reform has been led by a subcommittee of the college's curriculum committee. Their first decision was to use a zero-based approach to curriculum; that is, all general education courses would need to be formally proposed and reviewed. Subsequently, departments met to consider what they might offer to the new general education curriculum. By spring 1994, the task force had reviewed a number of course proposals and prepared a draft grid, or matrix, of how course proposals addressed the student competencies. Results were reviewed by a collegewide forum in the fall of 1994. It is an inductive approach to curriculum whereby course proposals lead to faculty decisions about the overall design of the curriculum.

The benefits of campus conversation range beyond creation of a new curriculum. Faculty say that curriculum discussions have been the best ever held at their college. They have talked about the nature of their disciplines and their relevance to themes of the MNTC. New pedagogy and possibilities for assessment are common topics in faculty discussions on campus. Recently, the entire staff development committee attended a national conference on teaching and learning. Within the next few months this college's general education curriculum will take shape for the fall of 1995, a shape already referred to by some as the best possible *first* step. They add that the focus on student learning establishes the right direction for the future.

General Education Reform in a Small College. According to one long-time faculty member, this small-town college had done general education reform before but always one discipline at a time. For this revision of the whole curriculum, college faculty decided at the outset that no courses would be "in"; all would have to earn a place in the new curriculum. In planning the new curriculum, faculty have been led by an ad hoc group (all of whom are members of the college curriculum committee) that meets weekly. All faculty were invited to well-attended conversations on general education scheduled in the afternoons from 3:00 to 5:00.

The committee goal in the first year was to establish a tentative framework for general education. Although their choice for that framework was the Traditional Model discussed earlier, for the first time they will be offering courses that address the competencies in the four theme areas of the MNTC. This is a significant step forward to a broader experience for students.

Challenges Remaining

The true test of this reform will be whether improvements in curriculum and student learning take hold and continue.

Continuing the Evolution. Faculty and academic administrators will continue to devise strategies and procure budgets to encourage, support, and reward an evolutionary curriculum. Of the list of issues still to be addressed, the first one is assessment of student learning. Once the question, What is the point of general education? has been answered, faculty need to know that students are "getting the point." Because "how" we teach is largely "what" we teach, students who are to become questioners and investigators need many opportunities to apply new skills of intellectual inquiry. New structures, such as freshman seminars or learning communities, would further the goals of this general education reform.

Surviving in a Changing Environment. On July 1, 1995, three Minnesota higher education systems—the community colleges, state universities, and technical colleges—became one new entity, the Minnesota State Colleges and Universities. While new leadership supports the Minnesota Transfer Curriculum and its goals, pressing issues of merger and some campus consolidations will compete for faculty and administrators' attention. Some present leaders will move into the new merged system. Their support for faculty development and innovation will be essential for ongoing success. New questions will emerge as technical college programs seek transfer recognition and as a faculty oversight committee begins its work to monitor general education under the umbrella of student transfer.

Conclusion

The MNTC has proved to be a more effective approach to general education than its framers might have realized. It encourages and supports a wide range of responses, allowing for differing visions of general education content and structure. It is possible to implement cautiously, experimenting with new approaches and teaching methods. Yet the themes and their demands for interdisciplinary problem solving pull faculty toward innovation. Its focus on student learning demands connections that break down barriers, whether they be barriers of structure, ineffective teaching, or inappropriate content. As a design for continuing improvement, the MNTC has a good chance of making a difference for students in the technical and community colleges in Minnesota.

NANCY REGISTER WANGEN is the system director for program collaboration for Minnesota State Colleges and Universities and worked closely with faculty to develop the transfer curriculum.

The authors address the institutional context, goals, philosophy, external constraints, and assessment implications of the general education program at Piedmont Virginia Community College. They offer four pieces of advice for institutions beginning their work in general education—namely, ownership, turf, larger external connections, and curricular restructuring.

The Piedmont Virginia Community College Experience in General Education

Deborah M. DiCroce, David R. Perkins

Without question, Piedmont Virginia Community College's (PVCC) general education program is the singularly most defining aspect of its existence as a comprehensive community college. Indeed, the program reflects both the college's academic standards and the uniqueness of its service region. This chapter describes the PVCC experience in general education by (1) placing the general education program within an institutional context, (2) identifying programmatic goals and the philosophical impetus for their development, (3) providing an analysis of pertinent state initiatives and mandates, (4) outlining the assessment implications of the program, and (5) offering useful advice to institutions beginning their work in general education.

Institutional Context

Piedmont Virginia Community College is part of the Commonwealth of Virginia's comprehensive community college system, which was founded in 1966 and consists of twenty-three colleges strategically situated across the state. Mid-size by system standards, the college opened its doors in September 1972. It served 6,953 different credit students in 1993–94, with an annualized FTE of 1,965 and a fall 1993 headcount of 4,369.

Statistical Profile. Since 1988–89, the college has experienced an 11 percent increase in enrollment. Enrollment is expected to level off until 1996–97, when an unusually high percentage of high school graduates is projected to commence in-state postsecondary study. Recent shifts in state public policy suggest that Virginia community colleges will play a major role in responding to the enrollment demand.

At present, PVCC offers twenty-five associate degree and ten certificate programs. Of the associate degree programs, eleven are in the university-parallel/college transfer area with the remaining fourteen in the occupational/technical area. The Associate in Arts (AA) and Associate in Science (AS) are awarded to those students intending to transfer into four-year baccalaureate programs. The Associate in Applied Science (AAS), Certificate (C), and Career Studies Certificate (CSC) are awarded to students preparing for specific occupational/technical occupations.

In 1993–94, the college's student body was 63 percent women, 82 percent part time, and 15 percent minority. African Americans made up 12 percent of the student body. The average age of the students was thirty-one, though nineteen was the most frequent age. Approximately 11 percent required some form of developmental course work. Thirty-five percent of all students were enrolled in courses designed to transfer, and 75 percent of those students who officially matriculated into a degree program were enrolled in transfer courses. In May 1994, the college awarded 259 degrees and certificates, 53 percent of which were in the AA and AS areas. In response to specific training needs for area business and industry, the college served 2,409 employees with specialized, tailor-made credit and noncredit course offerings. Indeed, in the most fundamental ways, the college is typical of a comprehensive community college.

Relationship with the University of Virginia. In other ways, however, PVCC is atypical of community colleges. Its uniqueness emanates from the service area itself and its relationship with the University of Virginia. The college is located in a university town, nestled between Thomas Jefferson's home of Monticello and the University of Virginia. With the exception of some light industry, the area's economic development is driven by small-to-medium-size businesses. The university is the area's largest employer. Paradoxically, the college's service area can best be described as a community of extremes—with incredible wealth on the one hand and incredible poverty on the other.

The presence of the University of Virginia, especially, has had an impact upon the college's culture. Obviously, it both creates a segment of the community that is highly educated and enhances the quality of life of the community with rich cultural opportunities that an area of this size simply would not be able to access on its own. But the university's influence on PVCC is far more deep-seated than this.

As a selective research university, the University of Virginia has played a major role in shaping the transfer curriculum. PVCC faculty define the college's academic standards for transfer education largely through the undergraduate standards of the university. In fact, the college typically transfers more students to the University of Virginia than all the other twenty-two community colleges in Virginia combined, and, upon transfer, PVCC students do as well as the native university student. This transfer rate speaks more to the model partnership between the two institutions than to the proximity of location. As an aside, 34 percent of the college's full-time teaching faculty hold doctorates, and many of them were conferred at the university. No doubt atypical of most community colleges, PVCC faculty exhibit characteristics associated with four-year college faculty.

Programmatic Goals and Philosophical Impetus

The present general education program of Piedmont Virginia Community College grew out of a college report for regional accreditation some ten years ago. Based on a 1983–1984 *Fifth-Year Report* to the Commission on Colleges of the Southern Association of Colleges and Schools (Piedmont Virginia Community College, 1984), the college concluded that its then current general education program was not grounded in any clearly identified set of beliefs and, consequently, demonstrated neither breadth nor coherence in some curricula.

Publication of Position Paper on General Education. Led by a core of faculty from all areas of the curriculum, the college engaged in wide-ranging debate on general education. The result was a set of student-oriented outcome statements that identified and reflected the competencies and values the PVCC community believed to be important for its students. A position paper issued in September 1984 provided the philosophical impetus for defining the role of general education in the "PVCC experience." It states:

> The successful community college must provide an education for its graduates that results in citizens who are well prepared as workers. It must do more, however. The graduate of the successful community college is an active citizen who is informed about the issues of the day and who uses good judgment in voting on the issues; the graduate thinks clearly as well as acts responsibly; the graduate uses leisure time in a way that is valuable to the individual and to society. The successful graduate, then, is one who has a general education as well as one who has specialized skills for earning a living. [Piedmont Virginia Community College, 1984, p. 2]

With this rationale as an underpinning, the college cited seventeen particular general education skills and habits of mind that its curricula, both university-parallel/college transfer and occupational/technical, would seek to cultivate. These goal statements addressed the topics of communication skills and the role of language, creative and critical thinking skills, the cultural role of science and mathematics, multicultural diversity and the global village, the process of scholarship, the role of the arts, the social and economic impact of technology, the harmony of mind and body, the basis for ethical judgment and behavior, and learning as an exciting, lifelong activity.

Position Paper and Grants Development. Of course, several uses for the position paper were soon recognized. The most obvious was its value in serving as a basis for curriculum review. To what degree did the college's programs incorporate courses whose content and learning objectives addressed the expected general education outcomes? Less apparent perhaps, but equally valuable, the statement of values served as a basis for grants development to strengthen general education at PVCC.

State Grant. Between 1986 and 1991, the college was successful in receiving three grants for strengthening its general education program. The first, a broad-based, two-year project, was funded by the State Council of Higher Education for Virginia for academic years 1986–87 and 1987–88. Entitled "Enhancing General Education at Piedmont Virginia Community College, 1986–88" (Piedmont Virginia Community College, 1986), this grant supported faculty, curriculum, and library development for general education. It also allowed for a review of the contribution of nonclassroom activities to general education outcomes. Finally, it sought to enhance articulation of the college's transfer programs with the University of Virginia.

NEH Grants. Overlapping this activity in time was another project of greater magnitude. Two planning and development grants from the National Endowment for the Humanities (NEH) spanned 1986–87 through 1990–91. Entitled *Strengthening General Education Through the Humanities* (Piedmont Virginia Community College, 1987, 1991), these grants focused specifically on the role of humanities in general education. The projects resulted in the expansion of library humanities holdings, the addition of a full-time faculty member in philosophy/religion, a program of extracurricular activities carefully designed to enrich humanities education, and the use of faculty release time for study, travel, and course development.

Development of Humanities Course Sequence. However, the central outcome of the NEH grants was a coherent, team-taught, six-semester-hour, interdisciplinary humanities course that blends its instructional emphases on the art, architecture, literature, music, and philosophy of Western culture. First presented in fall 1988, the course has been systematically improved by teaching faculty over the course of the past seven years. It remains the centerpiece of PVCC's general education program.

Establishing the new course within the college's degree program was not an easy task. Initially, the project director believed that the new course would be included in all university-parallel/college transfer and occupational/technical programs. But opposition surfaced among faculty in occupational/technical curricula as well as many faculty teaching in the university-parallel/college transfer programs. Following lengthy and sometimes acrimonious discussion, the compromise was to require the humanities course sequence in the AS general studies program (which enrolls the largest proportion of transfer students) and strongly encourage it in the college's remaining AA and AS degree programs. The compromise also incorporated a humanities elective into the college's AAS degree programs, thus ensuring that all associate degree curricula have a humanities component. This understanding was implemented by 1987–88, and it essentially remains in effect today.

Analysis of Pertinent State Initiatives and Mandates

Because PVCC functions as part of the state's community college system (VCCS), a piece of its general education program is shaped by state initiative and mandate. The VCCS prescribes a working definition for general education and a table of discipline-specific distribution requirements differentiated by degree type. PVCC's general education program must fit within the confines of this VCCS policy. The VCCS's current working definition for general education is as follows: "General education is that portion of the collegiate experience which addresses the knowledge, skills, attitudes, and values characteristic of educated persons. It is unbounded by disciplines and honors the connections among bodies of knowledge. The following eight elements embody the essence of general education: communication; learning skills; critical thinking; interpersonal skills and human relations; computational and computer skills; understanding culture and society; understanding science and technology; and wellness (Virginia Community College System, 1994, Section 2.IV.C, p. 2A–5). All Virginia community colleges are required to incorporate this definition into their catalogues and to demonstrate practices in general education consistent with it.

College Explication of State Definition. PVCC's explication of this definition is adapted from its 1984 position paper. It is also displayed in the college catalogue in the form of eleven general education elements that students achieve through the PVCC experience in general education. According to these guidelines (Piedmont Virginia Community College, 1994, p. 28), students should be able to:

• Present knowledge in an orderly and intelligible fashion, in writing and in speech
• Demonstrate value for a lifelong process of intellectual and cultural growth
• Obtain, understand, and use quantitative information
• Demonstrate computer literacy and appreciate the role of computers in society
• Understand how and where the sciences are applied, including their application to environmental problems
• Value physical and emotional health
• Understand the relationship of a person to society
• Develop appreciation for the arts and learn to make aesthetic judgments
• Articulate a global perspective
• Develop critical thinking
• Demonstrate interpersonal skills

State Degree Distribution Requirements. PVCC's general education program must also be placed within the context of the VCCS's table of distribution requirements. These requirements are applicable to all associate degree programs and reflect the systemwide definition of general education cited earlier.

The current version of these requirements was adopted in fall 1991 as part of the systemwide reform effort in general education. PVCC meets or exceeds the state policy requirements.

College Emphasis in General Education. Table 7.1 displays the college's minimum requirements for its associate degrees in both the university-parallel/college transfer and occupational/technical program areas. These requirements provide the framework for incorporating the eleven elements of the PVCC experience in general education into the curriculum. In addition, most programs exceed these minimal expectations in one or another of the five identified categories of general education.

Fundamentally, the culture of the college itself encourages a collegiate climate in which all faculty are aware of the multiple connections between the courses they teach and general education learning outcomes. In addition, strategies for fostering these outcomes are regularly discussed at division and department meetings. Periodic program reviews ask faculty how general education objectives are being met. And the content of specific courses—for example, attention in English composition to writing, speaking, and critical thinking skills—explicitly encompasses the general education elements. The expectation of computer literacy is addressed through either an elective computing course or a competency examination administered prior to graduation. Finally, curriculum infusion initiatives—most recently in ethics and service learning—strengthen the PVCC experience in general education.

Table 7.1. Piedmont Virginia Community College Minimum Distribution Degree Requirements

	General Education	Minimum Number of Semester-Hour Credits		
		AA	AS	AAS
I.	English Composition	6	6	3
II.	Humanities/Fine Arts	6	6	3
	Foreign Language	8	0	0
III.	Social/Behavioral Sciences	12	9	6
IV.	Natural Sciences	8	8	0
	Mathematics	6	6	3
V.	Wellness	2	2	2
	Minimum General Education Total	**48**	**37**	**17**
	Other Requirements for Associate Degrees			
VI.	Student Development	1	1	1
VII.	Major Field Courses and Electives	16	27	47
	Minimum Total for Degree	**65**	**65**	**65**

Assessment Implications

To be sure, assessment of student achievement of general education outcomes is no easy task. PVCC's experience indicates that answering three basic questions greatly facilitates the process: What do we want to know about our students' knowledge of general education? What assessment measures will give us those answers? How will we use the information we obtain to make appropriate changes in the curriculum?

Defining the Outcomes. In its work in assessing general education, the college has found that it is important to identify specifically the questions to be addressed in assessment. Working through the college's assessment committee and selected faculty, PVCC attempts first to identify its expected outcomes, stated as much as possible in measurable, objective terms. For example, whether students can state the steps in the scientific method is far easier to assess than whether students understand how the sciences are applied.

Measuring Student Achievement. After defining outcomes, the college determines exactly what it wants to know about students' knowledge of a particular general education area. Specificity is again important. For example, Do program-placed students improve their critical thinking skills as they progress through their program? is a more efficacious (and interesting) question than Do our students think critically? Care must be taken to include faculty in the generation of questions; otherwise, subsequent assessment activities may not be seen as relevant to the improvement of classroom instruction.

Once the areas for inquiry are precisely identified, it is much easier to determine appropriate measurement tools. Using multiple measures that include external and locally developed instruments improves the chances that data will be accurate and useful. PVCC gathers data by means of student, graduate, and employer surveys; standardized tests of general education such as the Academic Profile, Watson-Glaser Critical Thinking Appraisal, and Community College Experiences Questionnaire; various faculty projects designed to determine achievement in such areas as writing or math skills; and assessment by outside evaluators.

Using the Data Results. Although seemingly a relatively simple process, using assessment data to improve the curriculum becomes quite complex when the data do not pinpoint precisely the curricular weakness. For example, in PVCC's survey of transfer students, some respondents indicated problems with the amount and complexity of reading required in their upper-level course work. What does one do with such information? Should faculty in transfer curricula be encouraged to increase the amount of reading for all students in their classes? What are the implications with respect to faculty autonomy? How would changing the reading requirements affect casual students who are taking one or two courses in that particular program? Is it the amount of reading per individual course that is causing the difficulty, or do many transfer students from community colleges begin full-time study at the senior institutions when previously they carried only a part-time load? Rather than solving problems, assessment in general education quite often leads to more unanswered questions and can, if results are not used wisely, lead to costly and disruptive curricular changes that fail to remedy the perceived weaknesses.

Finally, in using general education assessment data, it is important to recognize that such discussions are often politically charged and threatening to both faculty and administrators. On the other hand, failure to demonstrate that assessment activities result in improved instruction and enhanced student learning will quickly damage an assessment program. An assessment plan that includes faculty-initiated projects having a direct bearing on classroom teaching, simplified data collection procedures, and a process for regular follow-up of assessment findings will result in a general education assessment program that has value to both faculty and students.

Lessons Learned

Over the past ten years, Piedmont Virginia Community College has learned much about both the process and product of establishing a general education program. The lessons it has learned serve as useful advice for institutions beginning their work in general education. They fall into four categories—namely, ownership, turf, larger external connections, and restructuring.

Ownership. Collegewide faculty ownership is critically important to developing a general education program. The institution should deliberately involve occupational/technical, as well as traditional liberal arts, faculty at the onset. It should also identify a shared philosophical framework for the ensuing debate. For obvious reasons, "critical thinking" can effectively frame this debate.

Turf. Ownership aside, turf battles are inevitable. For example, occupational/technical faculty will be concerned about a general education core overpowering the specialized requirements of their degree programs. Faculty who teach courses in literature, art history, theater, and philosophy may well be concerned about the effect of a required interdisciplinary humanities series on enrollment in introductory courses in their disciplines. The institution should anticipate such battles as natural, again finding the common bond of its culture and values and, where possible, encouraging course choice in developing the conceptual framework for the general education program.

Larger External Connections. External connections to four-year institutions, as well as to such external entities as governing boards or state coordinating agencies, constitute key linkages early on for a successful general education program. In particular, the institution should rally the support of its primary transfer institutions, involving them in the development of the program to ensure course transferability and using them to help make the case to external entities.

Restructuring. Like it or not, defining an institution's general education program cannot be done piecemeal and is best accomplished within the larger framework of curricular restructuring. Among other things, the institution should define for itself the key curricular questions it hopes to address in its work in general education. Three likely such questions are: What should be the maximum number of hours for the associate degree, and what portion should be devoted to general education? What ramifications do the global forces of change have for a general education core? How should technology redefine the content and structure of general education course offerings? In its restructuring context, the institution should also incorporate into its general education work such curricular matters as the appropriateness and extent of a foreign language component, an international dimension, a computer literacy requirement, and an interdisciplinary approach. It should attempt to reconcile the conflicting demands of the specialized, occupational/technical areas and the general education core. It should reconsider the established canons of such general education courses as survey English and American literature and world history, and it should prepare students for an increasingly complex, techno-logical, and multicultural world.

In short, these key curricular restructuring questions and related matters serve as a powerful synthesis for an institution's work in general education. Indeed, as PVCC's lessons learned, they speak fundamentally to the essence of the task and issue a clarion call for action.

References

Piedmont Virginia Community College. *Application for Funds for Excellence Grant—Enhancing General Education at Piedmont Virginia Community College, 1986–88—to State Council of Higher Education for Virginia.* Charlottesville, Va., February 1986.

Piedmont Virginia Community College. *College Catalogue, 1994–95.* Charlottesville, Va., 1994.

Piedmont Virginia Community College. *Fifth-Year Report to the Commission on Colleges of the Southern Association of Colleges and Schools.* Charlottesville, Va., July 1984.

Piedmont Virginia Community College. *Final Report on Planning Grant for Strengthening General Education Through the Humanities to National Endowment for the Humanities.* Charlottesville, Va., August 1987.

Piedmont Virginia Community College. *Final Report on Strengthening General Education Through the Humanities to National Endowment for the Humanities.* Charlottesville, Va., July 1991.

Piedmont Virginia Community College. *General Education, Position Paper Number One.* Charlottesville, Va., September 1984.

Virginia Community College System. *Policy Manual.* Richmond, Va., 1994.

DEBORAH M. DICROCE *is president of Piedmont Virginia Community College in Charlottesville, Virginia.*

DAVID R. PERKINS *is dean of instruction and student services at Piedmont Virginia Community College in Charlottesville, Virginia.*

Shoreline Community College has established general education outcomes that guide the design of a coherent core of study for both academic transfer and vocational students. Interesting features of the general education program include integrated studies courses and learning communities.

The General Education Core at Shoreline Community College

Marie E. Rosenwasser

Founded in 1964, Shoreline Community College (SCC) is a state-funded, comprehensive community college and one of the thirty districts comprising the Washington community and technical college system, ten of which are in the greater Puget Sound region. Shoreline is located ten miles north of Seattle in a residential community. There are 155 full-time faculty and an average of 200 part-time faculty serving a student body of approximately 8,500 full- and part-time students for an annual FTE of 4,500 to 5,000 students.

As a comprehensive community college, Shoreline is guided by vision statements that address excellence, diversity, responsiveness, innovation, and leadership. It is striving to achieve goals related to student mastery of college-level content and skills, a multicultural perspective through curriculum infusion, and a system for assessing educational outcomes. Shoreline's student body is 60 percent female and about 85 percent Caucasian. Approximately 65 percent of the students are enrolled in academic transfer or developmental education courses, and 35 percent are in vocational programs such as those in the health occupations, industrial or science technology, business technology and computing, and criminal justice, to name a few.

Rationale for General Education Requirements

In its mission statement Shoreline dedicates itself to student success and promises "an environment of excellence which encourages students to reach their potential and enables them to graduate with competence and confidence in their skills and knowledge, appreciation for diversity, a respect for the past and an openness to the future, and a sense of responsibility for global issues and the natural environment" (*Shoreline Community College's Plan for a General Education Core Curriculum*, 1990, p.1). Four of its 1991 to 1995 institutional goals relate to implementing a strong general education program and assessing student outcomes.

These excerpts from the definition and rationale of the approved general education core curriculum (*Shoreline Community College's Plan for a General Education Core Curriculum*, 1990) illustrate the relationship between institutional mission and goals and the college's philosophy of general education. "General education . . . exposes students to both the content and method of major areas of human inquiry. Broadly based and embedded throughout the curriculum, the Shoreline Community College general education program strives to develop, integrate and expand the experiences, knowledge, skills, attitudes and values of students through enduring academic exploration so that they are able to grow and mature in the process of inquiry and deliberative decision making throughout their lives" (p. 4). The rationale declares:

> This core program, through a broad and integrated exposure to the humanities, social sciences, multicultural studies, and the natural sciences, is designed to foster cognitive habits of evaluation and expression so that students have the opportunity to prepare themselves for creatively mature, healthy, intellectual and aesthetic lives through: a) developing the powers of reasoning and judgment and the ability to retrieve information; b) understanding and evaluating, historically and philosophically, the culture of the western world from which our institutions' mores and values originate; c) gaining insight into the diverse cultures of a world shrinking to a global neighborhood . . . ; d) becoming informed citizens prepared to exercise their constitutional freedoms responsibly. [p. 4]

Learning outcomes, which follow from the philosophical underpinnings of the definition and rationale for general education, address crosscurricular skills, knowledge, and attitudes and values. In abbreviated form, the twenty outcomes are presented as follows (*Shoreline Community College's Plan for a General Education Core Curriculum*, 1990, pp.5–6):

I. Skills: Students will be able to demonstrate competence in communication, quantitative reasoning, general intellectual (critical thinking) and social functioning skills.
    A. Communication: Demonstrate ability to: (1) read, listen and interpret, and communicate through appropriate spoken or written forms of standard English; (2) recognize and critically examine attitudes and values expressed by others in oral and written form; and (3) interpret and/or create appropriate visual and auditory representations complementary to the ideas expressed in language.
    B. Quantitative Reasoning: Demonstrate ability to apply principles of mathematics and logic to understanding and interpreting quantitative information and problems.

C. General Intellectual Abilities: Demonstrate ability to: (1) acquire, understand, process, and draw conclusions from information using observation, analysis, interpretation, speculation, and evaluation; (2) identify problems and engage in problem solving using alternative answers; (3) learn new skills, new technologies and develop new ideas; (4) use basic research methods and apply current technologies to retrieve, evaluate, and use information.

D. Social Functioning: Demonstrate ability to: (1) understand and tolerate different viewpoints and behaviors; (2) understand gender and cultural differences and adapt to multicultural settings; (3) cooperate with, relate to, and work with others; (4) apply leadership skills and assess personal strengths and weaknesses as a leader; 5) take civic, social, and environmental responsibility appropriate to the community.

II. Knowledge: Students will be able to comprehend and demonstrate knowledge of the principles inherent in the general education curriculum and exhibit active awareness of the natural, social, and cultural environment through an understanding of:

A. Methods and principles of scientific inquiry, its technological contributions, and their impact on humans and their environment.

B. Human responses to historical issues, ideologies, and events as well as the philosophies of organized societies.

C. Implications of the growing global interdependence of diverse societies and cultures.

D. Finding value in the aesthetics of the arts across time and cultures.

E. Implications of sound health practices.

III. Attitudes and Values: Based on their knowledge of themselves, the students will demonstrate the capability for continued self-direction by:

A. Exhibiting the ability to function effectively under conditions of ambiguity, uncertainty, and conflict.

B. Identifying personal values and cultural mores and consciously employing these in ethical decision making.

Factors Influencing Design of the General Education Program

Although part of the college's original administrative structure integrated vocational programs into academic divisions and housed both academic and vocational faculty from the humanities, sciences, and social sciences in the same area, this structure did not automatically result in a strong and coherent core of general education and related instruction in all the degree and certificate programs. With a strong faculty and administration confident in what they were doing and proud of the college's excellent reputation, it took a combination of external and internal forces to stimulate reform of the general education core curriculum.

External Factors. The Northwest Association of Schools and Colleges (NASC), after an interim visit in 1987, recommended stronger compliance with its policy on general education and related instruction. This spurred the college to strengthen the coherency of the general education program and ensure its inclusion in transfer and vocational degree and two-year certificate programs in preparation for a full-scale self-study and evaluation visit in 1992. Another source of external influence was the development of the Washington Associate in Arts degree transfer agreement by the Inter-College Relations Commission. Additionally, the University of Washington began to restrict the courses it would accept as satisfying distribution requirements in the humanities, social sciences, and sciences.

Internal Factors. At Shoreline the new executive vice president, hired in 1986, and the new Humanities Division chair, hired in 1988, brought experience in reforming general education from other colleges. Faculty leaders were aware of national developments in general education reform and wanted to strengthen Shoreline's educational program by making it more outcomes oriented. In addition, faculty began to observe an increasing disparity between their expectations of entering students' basic skills and knowledge and students' readiness for college. After several years of growing frustration over the students' lack of preparation for college-level work, Shoreline implemented a required initial assessment and placement system in fall 1988. Today, students who register for more than five quarter credit hours or for any English or math class are required to complete the American College Testing (ACT) "Assessment of Student Skills for Entry Transfer" (ASSET) placement tests in the areas of reading, language usage, and math skills. Students who score in what the English faculty identify as the "decision zone/borderline English 101" may write an essay for reconsideration of placement.

Test results showed 30 to 40 percent of the entering students place below freshman composition and 40 to 50 percent below intermediate algebra. While these test results clearly demonstrated that students' basic skills needed improvement for college success, the faculty did not agree that they shared responsibility for remediation. The same sort of resistance was encountered when it came to incorporating college-level competencies in general education. The faculty agreed that it was important, but they were not convinced that they should have to incorporate instruction in general education into vocational programs or that students should be required to take a core of courses designed to strengthen their skills and knowledge.

Description of the General Education Program

Responsive to existing institutional degree requirements and the Northwest Association's accreditation standards, the college has developed a core of courses within its basic and distribution degree requirements that operationalizes the definition and rationale of general education and is guided by the twenty student learning outcomes cited earlier. Courses that satisfy the core component have been reviewed and approved by the General Education Committee and are published in the college catalogue and on regularly updated lists of "Approved General Education Core Courses."

Courses that satisfy the general education core requirements for the Associate in Arts and Sciences (AAS) transfer and many of the Associate in Applied Arts and Science (AAAS) vocational degrees include:

Communication Skills—ENG 101 Composition and Expository Prose, ENG 102 Composition and Language Concepts.

Quantitative Reasoning, Symbolic Logic—Either one mathematics course at or above Math 105 Pre-Calculus 1-Elementary Functions, or PHIL 120 Logic, or PHYS 110 Physics of Current Issues, which requires the same proficiency as the Math 105 course.

Multicultural Education (3–5 cr.)—Multicultural Issues, Diversity, and Communication in U.S. Society, Sociology of Minority Groups, Cultural Anthropology, Ethnic Urban Patterns, or Gender, Race, and Class.

Integrated Studies A and B—Includes five-credit individual courses and ten- to fifteen-credit learning community or combined courses, all of which are listed on the "Approved List of General Education Core Curriculum Courses," updated quarterly.

Physical Education (3 cr.)—Either Wellness, First Aid, and Safety, or a variety of fitness and activity classes.

Integrated Studies Courses and Learning Communities. Integrated studies courses are classified into two categories. Those in Group A are broad and interdisciplinary, such as Humanities 160W: Culture and Science, and always have writing as integral to both content and grading. Generally, these are five-credit classes that have been created or revised to meet the criteria for Integrated Studies Group A. Other examples include: Science, Civilization, and Human Creativity (NatSci 104W); Encounters with Vanished Lives (Geology 100W); European Literature (ENG 281W, 282W, 283W); Literature of the American West (ENG 208W); Epidemics and Culture (BIOSC 150W); and Civilization and Culture (HIST/HUM 111W, 112W, 113W). However, the integrated studies requirement can also be satisfied by completing a "learning community." These learning communities typically contain two to three general distribution courses in the social sciences, natural sciences, and/or humanities organized around a common theme, as with a recent learning community titled "Thinking Green," which combined Environmental Science, Introduction to Macroeconomics, and a college composition course.

Also broader than most traditional liberal studies courses, Integrated Studies Group B courses are interdisciplinary within a given division and do not require a writing (W) designation. Examples of Integrated Studies Group B courses include: Art History, Understanding and Appreciating Music, Environmental Science, Introduction to Drama, Introduction to Anthropology, Survey of Japanese Literature, History of the Pacific Northwest, History of Jazz,

History of Costume, Modern European History, International Studies, Philosophical Classics, Introduction to Political Science, and Lifespan Development. Currently almost sixty courses have been approved by the General Education Committee as meeting Integrated Studies Group B criteria.

Regardless of whether integrated studies courses are classified into Group A or Group B, they all have to meet these ten criteria: be introductory; be multidisciplinary and nonvocational in nature; demonstrate breadth (spanning time and cultures) rather than depth of knowledge from the traditional areas of liberal studies; show the integration of ideas from discipline to discipline; include instruction in information retrieval and use of original as well as secondary source materials; show the different methodologies used in the study of major areas of knowledge; concentrate on the major ideas of the disciplines being studied in each course; incorporate practice in the four skills areas and application of relevant attitudes and values; work toward the student's development of positive personal identity and social interaction; and integrate the research methods and procedures used in a variety of academic disciplines.

Transfer Degree Requirements. The number and nature of the credits required in this comprehensive core depend on whether the student is completing the Option A or Option B AAS degree. At Shoreline and other community colleges in Washington State the standard, or general, transfer associate degree that meets the requirements as specified in the Inter-College Relations Commission's articulation agreement is called the "Option A Associate in Arts and Science," while the transfer degree that is shaped to meet unique general undergraduate requirements at a specific baccalaureate institution is called the "Option B Associate in Arts and Science" degree. There are thirty-one quarter hour credits in the general education comprehensive core required for the Option A AAS degree, but ten fewer credits may be required of the student completing the Option B AAS degree, depending on requirements of the intended transfer institution. The general education core component of the Option A AAS degree can be summarized as follows:

Communication (10) + Quantitative (5) + Multicultural (3) + Integrated Studies (10) + Physical Education (3)

In addition, students complete forty quarter credits in humanities, intra-American studies, science, and social science distribution courses and twenty-two elective or pre-major credits. Students completing the Option B AAS degree usually complete five fewer credits in communication and integrated studies, respectively, as do those pursuing the AAAS degree.

Vocational Preparatory Degree Requirements. AAAS degree students complete the same, or very similar, general education core requirements as the AAS degree students. Depending on their vocational-technical (applied) degree requirements, students might be allowed to use nontransfer, but college level, vocational communications and quantitative reasoning courses. Some vocational programs with more than ninety-six credits have been granted permission to require only five of the normal ten integrated studies credits, and some programs identify a specific integrated studies course that all students must take. For example, nursing students take Psychology 204: Lifespan Development, and graphic design students take Art History. To comply with Northwest Association of Schools and Colleges requirements for "related instruction," all vocational degree and certificate students must also complete a minimum of twenty hours (two credits) in human relations. The communications, quantitative reasoning, and human relations content and skills may, with committee approval, be embedded in program courses.

Development and Implementation Process

Early in 1989, the executive vice president and instructional administrators formed the SCC General Education Task Force composed of five vocational, six academic transfer, two developmental education, one counseling, and one library faculty. The chairs of the Humanities and Social Sciences divisions served as administrative representatives. The three charges to the task force were to: (1) develop a rationale for and definition of general education at SCC; (2) identify and define common cumulative learning outcomes of general education for all students receiving two-year associate degrees; and (3) develop a curricular design with established standards that will enable students in transfer or vocational degree programs to achieve these learning outcomes.

The task force deliberated over several proposals and eight months later released to the faculty a plan that included a core requirement of five credits of communications, five in quantitative reasoning, five in multicultural education, and fifteen credits of integrated humanities, science, and social science college transfer–level courses that addressed the twenty student learning outcomes. This proposal was criticized because it increased the general education credits for every degree program, especially those of the vocational students who would have had to add ten to twenty credits beyond their existing program requirements.

After a quarter of faculty forums and meetings with vocational advisory committees, the General Education Task Force revised the plan by reducing the total number of credits, while maintaining a commitment to a core of courses that integrated liberal arts knowledge and skills. The final proposal for the core curriculum was approved by the board of trustees in March 1990 and consists of the requirements identified earlier.

Creation of the General Education Implementation Committee. Once the general plan had been approved, the vice president formed the General Education Implementation Committee. Membership included some of the faculty and both division chairs from the original task force plus additional faculty and chairs from divisions with several vocational programs. This committee was asked to develop the implementation schedule, the process for identifying which courses would satisfy each of the categories of requirements, a process for hearing requests for exceptions for certain programs, and recommendations for how students would be informed of the changes and faculty advisers would be trained. Unlike the original General Education Task Force, which was ad hoc to the executive vice president, this committee reported to the Division Chairs Group, composed of all instructional administrators and chaired by the vice president, who then presented all degree changes and new course proposals to the College Cabinet for approval and adoption.

In fall 1990, the General Education Implementation Committee, Division Chairs Group, and vice president for academic affairs asked faculty to develop master course outlines for all courses that addressed relevant general education outcomes. Beginning with existing course outlines and class syllabi, faculty updated almost all the course outlines for the college curriculum. In its first year of implementation work, the committee struggled to specify and articulate criteria for Integrated Studies Group A and Group B and multicultural education requirements. At the same time, this committee realized that there were very few courses that met the criteria for Integrated Studies Group A or multicultural education. Therefore, the committee invited faculty to propose courses that combined content from broad fields of study, and with small curriculum development stipends, five such courses were developed.

Concurrently, faculty were also invited to demonstrate through revised course outlines how traditional liberal arts and sciences transfer courses could qualify as Integrated Studies Group A or Group B courses. The same process was used for considering individual courses or learning communities that would meet the requirements in communication skills, quantitative reasoning, or multicultural education.

All students entering Shoreline in fall 1992 were obliged to meet new graduation requirements in general education. Programs that admitted many transfer students, such as Dental Hygiene, took special measures to notify the advising offices at each college in the state about the new general education program. To facilitate the advising process and the evaluation of transfer students' general education courses, a handbook with criteria and master course outlines for general education core courses was developed.

The work of implementation continues. Committee membership has changed, and the General Education Implementation Committee is now called the General Education III Committee. This committee hears requests for exceptions to general education core requirements, recommends courses or learning communities that qualify as integrated studies or multicultural education, and shares membership and work related to curriculum and student learning with the campus committees on outcomes assessment, learning communities, and writing (W) courses. In fact, through General Education III, discussion about creating a standing college curriculum and outcomes assessment committee is beginning.

Assessment of General Education Core Curriculum Plan

There are two dimensions to the assessment process: the first is an evaluation of whether and how well the plan itself is operating, and the second is an assessment of the degree to which students are accomplishing the twenty general education student learning outcomes. The General Education Core Curriculum requirements have been in place for two academic years, and implementation has been smoother than many predicted. The annual college catalogue includes a list of degree requirements and courses that satisfy them; the quarterly class schedule is constructed to offer both day and evening students several opportunities for meeting the general education core requirements; faculty have been hired or trained to teach the multicultural education courses; more learning community courses are taught; the list of approved integrated studies and "W" courses is growing; and every degree or certificate program planning sheet identifies the required and recommended general education core courses. Generally, the plan is working well for those students who begin and complete their associate degrees at Shoreline.

Assisting transfer students, however, is proving challenging, particularly for the requirements in integrated studies and multicultural education. Some division chairs and the academic vice president spend more time evaluating students' transfer courses than they did prior to the implementation of the general education core curriculum requirements. Communication to advisers and other colleges about changes in the "Approved General Education Core Curriculum List" occurs regularly, but challenges in getting students and faculty advisers to understand and follow the degree plans remain.

Efforts to assess student attainment of the general education outcomes have begun. In response to a legislative mandate to assess institutional effectiveness, the Higher Education Coordinating Board directed all colleges and universities to develop and implement an outcomes assessment plan. Campus activity in outcomes assessment has involved substantial numbers of faculty and a variety of assessment strategies. Cross-disciplinary groups of faculty work to articulate more specifically each of the general education outcomes and propose ways to assess achievement of them. This work is leading to reshaping the outcomes and recognition of the need to assess the degree to which integration of knowledge and skills is occurring for students. Although clarifying the outcomes for communications is proving easier than those for quantitative reasoning, social functioning in multicultural society, and integrating knowledge, the faculty are beginning to develop a resource guide that articulates the skills and knowledge necessary to achieve the general education outcomes together with assessment techniques applicable to most courses. Evaluation methods such as portfolio assessment and focus group interviewing have been implemented, but use of a standardized test to assess the degree to which graduating students have achieved the general education outcomes has not yet been considered.

Lessons Learned

Lessons learned fall into the following categories: committee formation, campus participation, institutional research, student learning outcomes, size and complexity, communication and publication, and assessing outcomes.

Committee Formation. To achieve full and informed participation by all committee members, specify their responsibilities for keeping their division informed about committee deliberations and representing division viewpoints to the committee. Provide resources and training for members. To make the adoption phase smoother, make the process inclusive of faculty with a diversity of opinions about general education and from a range of academic and vocational programs. Counseling and library faculty should also be included.

Campus Participation. There must be lots of it, but not so much that the committee cannot get its work done. Invite nonmembers to attend meetings, to be part of focus groups, to give written input. Seek input from students. Keep the president and vice presidents informed, as their support is critical. Support from both Instruction and Student Services is needed if implementation of a general education core curriculum is going to succeed.

Institutional Research. Either before, or early in the process, gather information on degrees awarded, program requirements, where students transfer, students' course enrollment patterns, completion and retention rates, expectations for student learning as stated in course outlines, and the like. Such information will assist the committee as it struggles with shaping a general education core and anticipating problems in its implementation.

Student Learning Outcomes. Articulate outcomes expected of all students, and let the outcomes guide the curriculum design. The clearer faculty are in articulating general education outcomes, the easier it will be to shape the curriculum that addresses these outcomes and the assessment system that evaluates the degree to which students achieve them. Clearly articulated general education outcomes and course expectations should become part of master course outlines and class syllabi.

Size and Complexity of General Education Core Requirements. Be realistic about the number of credits that can be added to or used to replace degree requirements; avoid the temptation of ending "turf" wars by adding credits from everyone's department. Keep the core simple; creating two groups (that is, Integrated Studies Group A and Group B) of liberal studies courses leads to confusion. If integration of content and skills is part of the college's definition of general education, consider using clusters of courses, as in learning communities, to satisfy this objective, or requiring the same two to four general education courses of all students.

Communication and Publications. Develop a system for the committee to communicate with the campus on a regular basis. Develop student and faculty advising materials; use the catalogue, class schedule, program planning sheets, and brochures to warn of impending changes, as well as for implementation of new requirements.

Assessing Outcomes. Begin faculty work on articulating the skills and abilities needed for achievement of the student learning outcomes during the development of the curricular design. Engage faculty in assessing the degree to which important concepts such as "integrated learning" are achieved. Connect institutional research and outcomes assessment to curriculum reform.

Keep Learning. Although general education reform consumes time, avoid the temptations of implementing new requirements and not evaluating the results. Revising general education core requirements is best described as "work in progress."

Reference

Shoreline Community College's Plan for a General Education Core Curriculum. Core Curriculum Committee, Seattle, WA: Shoreline Community College, 1990.

MARIE E. ROSENWASSER is vice president for academic affairs and professor of speech and ESL at Shoreline Community College, Seattle.

Concluding Remarks

George Higginbottom

The eight curriculum models presented in this volume are products of the current wave of general education reform. Whatever their particular institutional needs or program designs, each has been deeply influenced by three seemingly disparate projects: *Harvard's Report on the Core Curriculum* (Harvard Committee, 1978), an update on the perennial quest for the liberally well-educated person; Miami-Dade's curriculum reform initiative, *General Education in a Changing Society* (Lukenbill and McCabe, 1978), aimed at making community college education count for something, while also being accountable; and Boyer and Levine's, *A Quest for Common Learning* (1981), which reminds us of our common humanity and the ties that bind people who are outwardly different. Taken together, these three projects have set general education reform's agenda concerning, for example, the individual and the community, social responsibility and freedom, and the means and ends of inquiry and knowledge.

Besides Boyer, Levine, and Lukenbill, other influential theorists and publicists of the contemporary reform effort, whose work has been especially important for community colleges, include Johnson (1952, 1982), Cohen and Brawer (1982, 1987), Collins and Drexel (1976), Case (1983), Gaff, as author (1983, 1991) and as editor of the American Association of College's GEM (General Education Models Project, 1979–1982), and Miller (1988).

What has inspired the work of these thinkers and curriculum reformers is the conviction that undergraduate education ought to be purposeful and edifying and that a portion of it ought to provide the grounding for broadly inclusive civic conversation. College educators, they argue, should define clearly and justify to each other what is essential to a college education, as well as prescribe a common set of learning objectives encompassing knowledge, cognitive and performative capabilities, the capacity for moral judgment, and dispositions of intellect and temperament. Furthermore, these learning goals should have a practical purport, enabling generally educated graduates to cope successfully with the myriad challenges of contemporary living and, in particular, with the requirements of competent, participative citizenship.

Although these contemporary reformers have advocated a more coherent general education for all levels of postsecondary education, each has acknowledged that the collision of perspectives and interests within and among diverse institutions would precipitate a variety of objectives and curricular content. Universities, for example, influenced by graduate school values and faculty research interests, would most likely favor a general education plan based upon established academic disciplines and their unique modes of intellectual inquiry. Liberal arts colleges, presumably more student-centered, would have greater latitude in certifying general education courses according to broadly shared criteria or in experimenting with thematic cross-disciplinary offerings. The most pragmatic of postsecondary institutions, community colleges would need to balance the interests of occupational and transfer-oriented curricula and faculty, lest general education goals be too abstract or, worse, misappropriated in the service of a narrow vocationalism.

Given such differences, what seems most remarkable after roughly fifteen years of general education reform is the extraordinary convergence of aims and objectives across these diverse postsecondary institutions. Whether impelled by political pressures for accountability, as is the case with most public colleges, or merely by an interest in rationalizing the knowledge and information explosion, or by concerns for stemming cultural splintering, agreement on the importance of enhanced thinking and communication skills, cultural (and multicultural) literacy, moral reasoning and judgment, and democratic citizenship spans the entire range of institutions. And that is especially true of community colleges, as our eight model programs attest.

Reviewing the learning goals endorsed by these eight community colleges, what patterns can be discerned? First, every college affirms the importance of clear communication. Composition courses and writing across the curriculum efforts have become the norm, and emphasis upon competence in oral discourse is increasingly common. Second, appreciation for diversity, multiculturalism, and global perspective characterizes all these programs. These commitments reflect recognition of and support for the diverse community college student constituency, as well as sensitivity to the social, cultural, and international milieu that graduates will inhabit. Third, there is the attempt to come to terms with technology: to help students become technologically literate, usually construed in terms of electronic information literacy. Fourth, there seems to be a consensus on the role of mathematics in the general education curriculum; beyond competence in basic algebra is a utilitarian aim: helping students to understand and interpret media-purveyed statistical data. Fifth, most programs have adopted goals related to ethics, expressed as moral reasoning, social responsibility, valuing education, or character development. Finally, virtually all programs aim to improve students' capacity for critical thinking and judgment.

Strong Foundations

Perhaps the most sustained reform effort of general education inquiry to date has been Jerry Gaff's. In two significant books, as editor of the *GEM Newsletter*, and as catalyst and mentor of the Task Force on Strong Foundations in General Education of the American Association of Colleges and Universities, Gaff has greatly stimulated general education reform efforts nationwide. In his *New Life for the College Curriculum* (1991), he reported on trends in general education reform, finding that it had become a total programmatic undertaking permeating all aspects of postsecondary education. Although the various pressures of the academic culture "conspire to whittle down good ideas that call for significant change from the status quo" (p. 77), there are, Gaff believes, good reasons to persist in light of survey responses that report large increases in favorable attitudes toward general education by both faculty and administrators as a consequence of reform efforts.

One development in general education reform reported by Gaff (1991, p. 73) is of particular interest to community college leaders who attempt to bridge the general-occupational education divide, namely, the growing popularity of approaches that seek "across the curriculum" learning objectives. Writing, critical thinking, appreciation for diversity, ethics and moral reasoning, and global perspective, for example, are objectives that can be accommodated within many existing courses and curricula. Instead of having to establish new core courses that draw off prospective students from traditional departmental offerings, skills and knowledge infusion approaches pose little threat to organizational arrangements and discipline integrity, requiring only modest changes in content areas but—and here is the most interesting part—major changes in instructional methodologies. General education so conceived is more than mere curriculum redesign; if done conscientiously and well, it focuses the attention of faculty squarely upon the quality of teaching and learning.

Most of the community colleges profiled in this volume have adopted, as much out of necessity as conviction, across the curriculum models that typically combine "core" courses—composition, science, a thematically organized offering—with across the curriculum course infusion. It is a practical solution to the internal and external strictures that beset community colleges. A general education program that proposes to be comprehensive must establish its objectives within the curricular constraints imposed by state education and university systems, accrediting and licensing agencies, and even employer preferences. With a sixty-plus credit hour limitation and an institutional mission and philosophy different from senior colleges, community college general education must attempt to prepare graduates for both seamless transfer to senior colleges and immediate employment. Hence the common recourse to across the curriculum infusion.

Among our eight contributors one also finds a common nomenclature for general education learning—outcome, proficiency, competency—that is decidedly more practical and technical than is the case at most senior colleges.

Blackhawk's DACUM, for example, is a method for writing curriculum goals and rendering them in performative language. Jefferson, in Kentucky, has been involved in drafting a systemwide set of competency statements, as have the Minnesota Community Colleges. Piedmont, in Virginia, established its campus outcome objectives within the statewide general education definition and discipline distribution framework. And even Shoreline, with more institutional autonomy, has developed a list of twenty learning outcomes that provide specificity for the skills, knowledge, and attitude commitments of its mission statement and general education definition.

Not only is the careful specification of outcomes, or competencies, a deeply ingrained practice at two-year institutions obsessed with accountability and performance (some community colleges have recently taken to certifying their graduates to employers) but it is also an effective means of installing general education objectives in across-the-curriculum infusion models. The practice ensures that desired learning outcomes are widely disseminated and that the learning goals themselves are assessable. The more difficult task, one requiring serious, ongoing faculty involvement, concerns the degree to which understanding is shared and commitment given.

That the general education reform process is a total, long-term undertaking is not the only cautionary advice offered by our authors. Another relates to the very practice of rendering general education objectives in behavioral language. Care must be taken to ensure that the specification of learning competencies does not unduly restrict divergent expression and that learning outcomes are not reduced only to what is measurable. Virtually all our eight colleges continue to speak the more subjective educational language of understanding, appreciation, and reflection while conscientiously developing general education learning goals and implementing assessment strategies.

Community College Models: Measuring Up

Although most colleges continue to struggle with general education assessment, there is evidence (Astin, 1993; Terenzini and Pascarella, 1991; Gaff, 1991) that comprehensive, firmly established, and strongly supported programs lead to enhanced student learning and degree persistence. The Strong Foundations Task Force, convened by Gaff in 1993, drew inspiration from those findings. Members worked to define a set of basic premises around which general education curricular reform ideally would coalesce. The task force (Project on Strong Foundations for General Education, 1994, pp. 3–54) proposed that effective general education programs (paraphrasing the text):

1. Are clear about their aims
2. Embody an institutional mission
3. Strive for coherence
4. Are committed to values education and social responsibility
5. Are attentive to students' experiences

6. Are constantly evolving
7. Are community-building projects
8. Require strong campus leadership at all levels
9. Have a diverse base of support
10. Promote cross-disciplinary dialogue
11. Suffuse the co-curriculum
12. Monitor and assess performance vis-à-vis an evolving vision

This group of affirmations constitutes a formal framework for general education curricular reform suitable for guiding the practice of all sorts of institutions, while also setting out some of the parameters of substantive debates over goals. It is a document of inclusion, equally germane to the diverse missions and clienteles of elite liberal arts colleges, state universities, and community colleges. These twelve statements seek curricular coherence based upon educational and institutional visions that are continuously evolving, that take students' experiences, interests, and needs (even learning styles) seriously, and that link curriculum with professional development and collegiality among all campus constituencies.

General education curricular reform so conceived can become a program for transforming institutions—their instructional methodologies, organizational structures, and human relationships—although, typically, the initial undertaking does not encompass such broad goals (Gaff, 1991). Few reformers, in fact, understand at the outset the capacity of general education reform to stimulate pedagogical conversation by disclosing teaching and learning issues that hitherto had been overlooked or avoided. These transformational consequences of general education reform are borne out again and again in the narratives of our eight community college authors. Manifestly, chapter authors have sought to be clear about their colleges and to align general education goals with the college's mission.

Emblematic of the similarity among our institutions is their common striving for what the "Strong Foundations" group termed educational coherence. With emphasis upon coherence, a formal property of program design, the object of curricular organization and student learning can assume several different arrangements; content, skills, inquiry, and personal development models, however different conceptually, share the same integrative aspirations. If our community college models tend to elevate cognitive and communication skills objectives over other visions of curricular coherence, it is only a matter of emphasis. None of the eight neglects content, inquiry, and personal development goals.

In varying degrees all eight institutions have adopted goals referencing social and civic responsibility, Jefferson, Shoreline, Minnesota, and Broome in particular. Always affected early by social, economic, and demographic changes, community colleges are attentive to characteristics of the student population that bear critically upon the general education program. Virtually all the models in this volume provide analyses of student attributes as contexts for curriculum planning. Those profiling their student bodies in greatest detail include Miami-Dade, Piedmont, and Bunker Hill.

That general education program development is open ended and evolving and that it is a community-building enterprise are richly textured discoveries of the process itself. Black Hawk's DACUM process is illustrative of the community-building aspect of curriculum reform, as is, notably, Shoreline's, Miami-Dade's, and Bunker Hill's. Broome and Miami-Dade seem to have committed most fully to integrating curricular and co-curricular learning goals, although all eight institutions have thematized lifelong learning as a focal aim of their programs.

Finally, each of these eight colleges has paid close attention to assessment: to what the "Strong Foundations" group represents as "Progress Toward an Evolving Vision Through Ongoing Self-Reflection (Project on Strong Foundations, p. 52). Difficulties inherent in assessing student learning within courses, across the curriculum, and over time are further complicated by the dynamic nature of general education program objectives. Although freely acknowledging these difficulties, our eight colleges remain steadfast in their efforts to determine whether demonstrable enhancements in student learning can be attributed to general education reform efforts.

The narratives and reflective appraisals of the authors featured in this volume recapitulate the experiences of all institutions that have embarked upon the long and difficult journey of general education curriculum development. Each of the "Strong Foundations" principles has special poignancy for these authors and their institutions, for they are connected in their experiences to specific issues, actors, debates, disagreements, resolutions, frustrations, and compromises. One is struck, nonetheless, by how similar their experiences have been. Authorial reports on "lessons learned," for example, amplify and extend the tenets of the "Strong Foundations" group, while also attesting not only to the similarity of community college culture but especially to the remarkable (and comforting) play of reasoned judgment.

Regional accrediting bodies seem also to have exerted powerful convergent influences on behalf of general education reform, even to the point of urging the adoption of specific learning goals and pedagogies. Systemwide efforts, such as those in Kentucky, Minnesota, and California, undertaken principally to smooth two-year/four-year transfer, have both positive and negative features, as our authors explain: loss of institutional autonomy and the eclipse of home-grown models—negatives—are balanced by standardization of requirements and predictability, which favor students. And while transfer talk is the common coin of systemwide bargaining, that dialogue usually spills over into occupational programs, and students in these curricula also benefit.

Given this account of similarity among our eight institutions and of convergence on general education goals within postsecondary education generally, one might wonder if this movement toward curricular commonality is becoming stultifying? Clearly not, for the tasks of specifying the content and learning protocols for each of the general education objectives are highly complex and intellectually engaging undertakings for faculty and staff. Innovative curriculum design and conversation on teaching and learning provide opportunities for all sorts of creative synergy and professional development. General education reform is full of surprises and provides many opportunities for personal growth. By sharing and disseminating this discourse on the goals of our common learning we improve our teaching, gain both credibility for and satisfaction in our intellectual and pedagogic practices, and, most important of all, help our students toward enlightened, competent participation in the ensemble of conversations, activities, and institutions that constitute our social being.

References

Astin, A. What Matters in College. San Francisco: Jossey-Bass, 1993.

Boyer, E. L., and Levine, A. A Quest for Common Learning. Washington, D.C.: The Carnegie Foundation for the Advancement of Teaching, 1981.

Case, C. "Reformulating General Education Programs." In G. B. Vaughan (ed.), Issues for Community College Leaders in a New Era. San Francisco: Jossey-Bass, 1983.

Cohen, A. M., and Brawer, F. The American Community College. San Francisco: Jossey-Bass, 1982.

Cohen, A. M., and Brawer, F. The Collegiate Function of Community Colleges. San Francisco: Jossey-Bass, 1987.

Collins, C. C., and Drexel, K. O. General Education: A Community College Model. Pittsburg, Calif.: Community College Press, 1976.

Gaff, J. G. General Education Today: A Critical Analysis of Controversies, Practices, and Reforms. San Francisco: Jossey-Bass, 1983.

Gaff, J. G. New Life for the College Curriculum: Assessing Achievements and Furthering Progress in the Reform of General Education. San Francisco: Jossey-Bass, 1991.

Gaff, J. G. (ed.) GEM Newsletter. Washington, D.C.: Project on General Education Models, 1979–1982.

Harvard Committee. Report on the Core Curriculum. Cambridge, Mass.: Office of the Dean, Faculty of Arts and Sciences, Harvard University, 1978.

Johnson, B. L. General Education in Action. A Report of the California Study of General Education in the Junior College. Washington, D.C.: American Council on Education, 1952.

Johnson, B. L. General Education in Two-Year Colleges. San Francisco: Jossey-Bass, 1982.

Lukenbill, J. D., and McCabe, R. H. General Education in a Changing Society. Dubuque, Iowa: Kendall/Hunt, 1978.

Miller, G. The Meaning of General Education: The Emergence of a Paradigm. New York: Columbia University Press, 1988.

Project on Strong Foundations for General Education. Strong Foundations: Twelve Principles for Effective General Education Programs. Washington, D.C.: Association of American Colleges, 1994.

Terenzini, E. T., and Pascarella, P. T. How College Affects Students. San Francisco: Jossey-Bass, 1991.

GEORGE HIGGINBOTTOM is dean of the Division of Liberal Arts and Related Careers at Broome Community College in Binghamton, New York. He is founding member and past president of the Community College General Education Association.

The editors cite additional references that match the most common learning goals mentioned in the eight general education plans in this volume.

Additional Sources of Information

George Higginbottom, Richard M. Romano

For a bibliography of material on general education, we refer the reader to the references at the end of each chapter. They contain most of the works that have informed the general education debate at the community college. In this chapter we will focus on a few additional sources of information. As we mentioned in the introductory chapter, a great degree of agreement as to what is important can be found among the general education plans at most campuses. For this reason we have concentrated on citing additional references that match up with the most common learning goals among these plans.

Civic Education

Although not all the colleges profiled in this volume have adopted formal goals in civic education, most acknowledge as general education aims the importance of competent, participative citizenship. Those wishing to learn more about the subject should consult B. Barber, *Strong Democracy: Participatory Politics for a New Age,* Berkeley, Calif.: University of California Press, 1984; R. Freeman Butts, *The Revival of Civic Learning,* Bloomington, Ind.: Phi Delta Kappa Foundation, 1980; S. W. Morse, *Renewing Civic Capacity: Preparing College Students for Service and Citizenship,* ASHE-ERIC Higher Education Report No. 8, Washington, D.C.: George Washington University Press, 1989; B. Murchland (ed.), *Higher Education and the Practice of Democracy: A Political Education Reader,* Dayton, Ohio: Kettering Foundation, 1991; R. Pratte, *The Civic Imperative: Examining the Need for Civic Education,* New York: Teacher's College Press, 1988; and F. M. Lappé, *The Quickening of America,* San Francisco: Jossey-Bass, 1994.

"The Civic Purposes of Liberal Learning," *Liberal Education,* winter 1982, contains a superb collection of essays on the subject. In addition to these are the numerous recent books and articles on community service as civic education. Finally, three organizations actively involved in promoting citizenship education are the National Council for the Social Studies, Washington, D.C., the Center for Civic Education, Calabasas, California, and the Kettering Foundation, Dayton, Ohio.

Communication

Community college general education programs in communication generally include reading, writing, listening, and speaking skills. Virtually all administer placement examinations to entering students in reading and writing; all require at least one composition course, and many also require a course in public speaking or oral communication. Since English faculty generally keep abreast of the literature in composition theory, the following references address communicating across the curriculum. Writing across the curriculum, or disciplines, is a broadly shared goal of higher education.

Writing Across the Curriculum in Community Colleges, L. C. Stanley and J. Ambron (eds.), New Directions for Community Colleges, no. 73, San Francisco: Jossey-Bass, 1991, is a fine resource that reviews the movement, explores its theoretical foundations, and presents a great many "how-to" strategies. Its end-of-chapter references and bibliography are indispensable for those seeking guidance in not only written communication but also critical thinking and "writing-to-learn" pedagogy. Of the journal and periodical literature College English and College Composition and Communication provide rich resources for practitioners.

Critical Thinking

The spiritual and intellectual center of the critical thinking movement is Richard Paul's Sonoma State University Center for Critical Thinking and Moral Critique. Its stimulating August conferences attract many of the leaders of the movement. The center has also spawned regional organizations and workshops. Available from the center are instructional videos and print materials. Other centers of important critical thinking programs are the Oakton (Illinois) Critical Literacy Project and the Montclair (New Jersey) State University Institute for Critical Thinking.

The following texts are essential reading for faculty and institutions serious about critical thinking. Introductions to the topic, its theoretical grounds and disagreements, include J. Kurfiss, Critical Thinking: Theory, Research, Practices, and Possibilities, ASHE-ERIC Higher Education Report No. 4, Washington, D.C.: Clearinghouse on Higher Education, 1988; A. Benderson, "Critical Thinking," FOCUS, Princeton, N.J.: Educational Testing Service, 1984; R. Paul (ed.), "Critical Thinking," National Forum, winter 1985, Baton Rouge, La.: Honor Society of Phi Kappa Phi, Louisiana State University. Richard Paul's Critical Thinking: What Every Person Needs to Survive in a Rapidly Changing World, Santa Rosa, Calif.: Foundation for Critical Thinking, 1994, is a treasure trove of essays on the subject. Cynthia Barnes (ed.), Critical Thinking: Educational Imperative, New Directions for Community Colleges, no. 77, San Francisco: Jossey-

Bass, 1992, and R. E. Young (ed.), *Fostering Critical Thinking,* San Francisco: Jossey-Bass, 1980, provide helpful strategies on a wide range of matters from instruction to assessment. Among other important works are J. Chaffee, *Thinking Critically,* Boston: Houghton-Mifflin, 1991 (a text); V. R. Ruggiero, *The Art of Thinking: A Guide to Critical and Creative Thought,* New York: Harper-Collins, 1991; and V. R. Ruggiero, *Teaching Thinking Across the Curriculum,* New York: Harper and Row, 1988; S. Brookfield, *Developing Critical Thinkers,* San Francisco: Jossey-Bass, 1987; and M. Lipman, *Thinking in Education,* Cambridge, England: Cambridge University Press, 1991.

Ethics

Despite the current clash of moral theories—cognitive developmental, virtue and value based, and feminist—some form of moral education appears to be a goal of virtually all general education programs. As heightened ethical consciousness has become integral to education in the professions, health sciences, engineering, and business curricula, texts increasingly incorporate discussions on relevant moral dilemmas.

Those wishing to explore the bases of moral psychology and philosophy should consult the many works of Lawrence Kohlberg in cognitive moral development. T. Likona, *Education for Character: How Our Schools Can Teach Respect and Responsibility,* New York: Bantam, 1992; E. A. Wynne, "The Great Tradition in Education: Transmitting Moral Values," *Educational Leadership,* December 1985/January 1986, 43(4) p. 4–9; C. Hoff Sommers, "Ethics Without Virtue," *The American Scholar,* summer 1984; and the books and articles of William Bennett are excellent on character education.

For feminist ethics see C. Gilligan, *In a Different Voice: Psychological Theory and Women's Development,* Cambridge, Mass.: Harvard University Press, 1982; and N. Noddings, *Caring: A Feminine Approach to Ethics and Moral Education,* Berkeley, Calif.: University of California Press, 1984. A "how-to" brief text with case studies by V. R. Ruggiero, *Thinking Critically About Ethical Issues,* San Francisco: Mayfield, 1992, is a useful supplement to course texts.

International/Intercultural Education

The terms "international" or "global studies" most often refer to the diversity of political, economic, and cultural issues outside the United States. For information on this, readers can start with R. K. Greenfield (ed.), *Developing International Education Programs,* New Directions for Community Colleges, no. 70, San Francisco: Jossey-Bass, 1990. It contains a wealth of references and information, not just on curriculum matters but also on other aspects of internationalizing the campus. For profiles of campus programs see "Internationalizing the Curriculum," *The Forum for International Education,* March 1984, 6 (4); and *Beyond Borders: Profiles in International Education,* Washington, D.C.: Association of American Colleges and Universities, 1994.

The terms *multiculturalism* and especially *diversity* direct attention to multiethnic, racial, and gender issues within the United States. Fifteen to twenty years ago colleges talked about introducing global dimensions into the curriculum. This has gained widespread acceptance among both four- and two-year colleges. Now the debate has shifted to whether diversity should be included in the general education curriculum. We could find very few cases where community colleges have actually done this, and where they have, it has tended to be an infusion effort. The leaders in introducing diversity into the curriculum are located in border states, such as California, Texas, Florida, and Washington, for obvious reasons. Four-year colleges seem to be more aggressive in introducing diversity requirements than two-year colleges.

The literature on diversity is vast. For a recent discussion relevant to general education see G. H. Cornwell and E. Stoddard, "Things Fall Together," *Liberal Education,* Fall 1994, *80* (4), pp. 40–51. For an examination of theoretical and practical issues in multicultural curricula see B. Schmitz, *Core Curriculum and Cultural Pluralism: A Guide for Campus Planners,* Washington, D.C.: Association of American Colleges, 1992.

Mathematics, Science, Technology

Most community colleges have established standards of mathematical or quantitative proficiency. These usually entail familiarization with concepts and methods of data analysis aimed at enhancing graduates' competencies as citizens, workers, and problem solvers. A trend in science education is to require both biological and physical science course work. In many community colleges technological literacy is interpreted as computer literacy: the ability to use a computer for word processing, data manipulation, and problem solving and, increasingly, for becoming "information literate." Where general education reform has provoked innovative thinking, new course development in technological literacy has taken several forms: historical/topical surveys; science, technology, and society problems courses; and across the curriculum course integration.

One of the most ambitious of the survey type is offered at Johnson County (Kansas) Community College which combines a historical overview with units on Energy and Society, Electronics and Computers, Transportation, Materials, and Assessment. Such courses present opportunities for collaboration among scientists, engineers, philosophers, and social scientists at community colleges. With growing anxieties about economic competitiveness together with a gathering consensus on worksite skills, such courses are likely to multiply.

Journals

Journals that feature general education issues include *The Journal of General Education,* Pennsylvania State University Press, University Park, Penn.; *Perspectives,* Journal of the Association of General and Liberal Studies, Columbus, Ohio; and *Liberal Education,* Journal of the American Association of Colleges and Universities, Washington, D.C.

INDEX

Ordering Information

New Directions for Community Colleges is a series of paperback books that provides expert assistance to help community colleges meet the challenges of their distinctive and expanding educational mission. Books in the series are published quarterly in Spring, Summer, Fall, and Winter and are available for purchase by subscription and individually.

Subscriptions for 1995 cost $49.00 for individuals (a savings of more than 25 percent over single-copy prices) and $72.00 for institutions, agencies, and libraries. Please do not send institutional checks for personal subscriptions. Standing orders are accepted. (For subscriptions outside of North America, add $7.00 for shipping via surface mail or $25.00 for air mail. Orders *must be prepaid* in U.S. dollars by check drawn on a U.S. bank or charged to VISA, MasterCard, or American Express.)

Single copies cost $19.00 plus shipping (see below) when payment accompanies order. California, New Jersey, New York, and Washington, D.C. residents please include appropriate sales tax. Canadian residents add GST and any local taxes. Billed orders will be charged shipping and handling. No billed shipments to post office boxes. (Orders from outside North America *must be prepaid* in U.S. dollars by check drawn on a U.S. bank or charged to VISA, MasterCard, or American Express.)

Shipping (Single Copies Only): one issue, add $3.50; two issues, add $4.50; three issues, add $5.50; four to five issues, add $6.50; six to seven issues, add $7.50; eight or more issues, add $8.50.

Discounts for quantity orders are available. Please write to the address below for information.

All orders must include either the name of an individual or an official purchase order number. Please submit your order as follows:
    Subscriptions: specify series and year subscription is to begin
    Single copies: include individual title code (such as CC82)

Mail all orders to:
    Jossey-Bass Publishers
    350 Sansome Street
    San Francisco, California 94104-1342

For subscription sales outside of the United States, contact any international subscription agency or Jossey-Bass directly.

OTHER TITLES AVAILABLE IN THE
NEW DIRECTIONS FOR COMMUNITY COLLEGES SERIES
Arthur M. Cohen, Editor-in-Chief
Florence B. Brawer, Associate Editor

UNITED STATES POSTAL SERVICE

Statement of Ownership, Management, and Circulation
(Required by 39 U.S.C. 3685)

1. Publication Title: NEW DIRECTIONS FOR COMMUNITY COLLEGES
2. Publication No.: 0 1 9 4 3 0 8 1
3. Filing Date: 9/22/95
4. Issue Frequency: Quarterly
5. No. of Issues Published Annually: Four (4)
6. Annual Subscription Price: $49.00 (personal) $72.00 (institution)
7. Complete Mailing Address of Known Office of Publication (Street, City, County, State, and ZIP+4) (Not Printer): 350 Sansome Street, 5th Floor, San Francisco, CA 94104-1342 (San Francisco County)
8. Complete Mailing Address of Headquarters or General Business Office of Publisher (Not Printer): (above address)
9. Full Names and Complete Mailing Addresses of Publisher, Editor, and Managing Editor (Do Not Leave Blank)
Publisher (Name and Complete Mailing Address): Jossey-Bass Inc., Publishers (above address)
Editor (Name and Complete Mailing Address): Arthur M. Cohen, ERIC Clearinghouse for Junior Colleges, School of Education UCLA, 3051 Moore Hall, 405 Hilgard Ave, Los Angeles, CA 90024-1521
Managing Editor (Name and Complete Mailing Address): Lynn D. Luckow, President, Jossey-Bass Inc., Publishers (address above)

10. Owner (If owned by a corporation, its name and address must be stated and also immediately thereafter the names and addresses of stockholders owning or holding 1 percent or more of the total amount of stock. If not owned by a corporation, the names and addresses of the individual owners must be given. If owned by a partnership or other unincorporated firm, its name and address as well as that of each individual must be given. If the publication is published by a nonprofit organization, its name and address must be stated.) (Do Not Leave Blank.)

Full Name	Complete Mailing Address
Simon & Schuster, Inc.	PO Box 1172
	Englewood Cliffs, NJ 07632-1172

11. Known Bondholders, Mortgagees, and Other Security Holders Owning or Holding 1 Percent or More of Total Amount of Bonds, Mortgages, or Other Securities. If none, check here. ☐ None

Full Name	Complete Mailing Address
same as above	same as above

12. For completion by nonprofit organizations authorized to mail at special rates. The purpose, function, and nonprofit status of this organization and the exempt status for federal income tax purposes: (Check one)
☐ Has Not Changed During Preceding 12 Months
☐ Has Changed During Preceding 12 Months
(If changed, publisher must submit explanation of change with this statement)

PS Form 3526, October 1994 (See Instructions on Reverse)

13. Publication Name: NEW DIRECTIONS FOR COMMUNITY COLLEGES (CC)
14. Issue Date for Circulation Data Below: CC 89 (Spring 1995)

15. Extent and Nature of Circulation	Average No. Copies Each Issue During Preceding 12 Months	Actual No. Copies of Single Issue Published Nearest to Filing Date
a. Total No. Copies (Net Press Run)	1900	1500
b. Paid and/or Requested Circulation (1) Sales Through Dealers and Carriers, Street Vendors, and Counter Sales (Not Mailed)	67	61
(2) Paid or Requested Mail Subscriptions (Include Advertisers' Proof Copies/Exchange Copies)	858	782
c. Total Paid and/or Requested Circulation (Sum of 15b(1) and 15b(2))	925	843
d. Free Distribution by Mail (Samples, Complimentary, and Other Free)	215	230
e. Free Distribution Outside the Mail (Carriers or Other Means)	0	0
f. Total Free Distribution (Sum of 15d and 15e)	215	230
g. Total Distribution (Sum of 15c and 15f)	1140	1073
h. Copies Not Distributed (1) Office Use, Leftovers, Spoiled	354	427
(2) Return from News Agents	6	0
i. Total (Sum of 15g, 15h(1), and 15h(2))	1500	1500
Percent Paid and/or Requested Circulation (15c / 15g x 100)	81%	79%

16. This Statement of Ownership will be printed in the CC92/Fall95 issue of this publication. ☐ Check box if not required to publish.

17. Signature and Title of Editor, Publisher, Business Manager, or Owner: Sue Lewis, Director of Periodicals   Date: 9-18-95

I certify that all information furnished on this form is true and complete. I understand that anyone who furnishes false or misleading information on this form or who omits material or information requested on the form may be subject to criminal sanctions (including fines and imprisonment) and/or civil sanctions (including multiple damages and civil penalties).

Instructions to Publishers

Complete and file one copy of this form with your postmaster on or before October 1, annually. Keep a copy of the completed form for your records.

Include in items 10 and 11, in cases where the stockholder or security holder is a trustee, the name of the person or corporation for whom the trustee is acting. Also include the names and addresses of individuals who are stockholders who own or hold 1 percent or more of the total amount of bonds, mortgages, or other securities of the publishing corporation. In item 11, if none, check box. Use blank sheets if more space is required.

Be sure to furnish all information called for in item 15, regarding circulation. Free circulation must be shown in items 15d, e, and f.

If the publication had second-class authorization as a general or requester publication, this Statement of Ownership, Management, and Circulation must be published; it must be printed in any issue in October or the first printed issue after October, if the publication is not published during October.

In item 16, indicate date of the issue in which this Statement of Ownership will be printed.

Item 17 must be signed.

Failure to file or publish a statement of ownership may lead to suspension of second-class authorization.

PS Form 3526, October 1994 (Reverse)